# WOMEN ON THE MARCH

## AUTHOR'S NOTE

The armed services are aware that job titles (radioman, corpsman and bandsman, for example) and other military terms do not always reflect the equal status of the military woman, and changes will be made as new regulations and manuals are issued.

In the case of terms indicating rank, such as *Airman, First Class,* congressional legislation is involved and changes will take longer. In WOMEN ON THE MARCH we have employed the terminology used by the armed forces at the time the book was written.

# WOMEN ON THE MARCH

## GENE and CLARE GURNEY

Illustrated with photographs

ABELARD-SCHUMAN
*New York*

Designed by Stanley S. Drate

**Library of Congress Cataloging in Publication Data**

Gurney, Gene
   Women on the march.

   SUMMARY: Describes job opportunities for women in the armed forces and briefly traces the history of their changing role.

   1. United States—Armed Forces—Women—Juvenile literature. 2. Military service as a profession—Juvenile literature. [1. United States—Armed Forces—Women. 2. Military service as a profession] I. Gurney, Clare, joint author. II. Title.
UB147.G87        355'.0023        73-18546
ISBN 0-200-00132-9

Manufactured in the United States of America

10 9 8 7 6 5 4 3 2 1

# CONTENTS

*List of Illustrations* 7

**1** A Ceremony for Promotion 9

**2** Some Women Who Went to War 24

**3** A Choice Worth Considering 45

**4** Women on the March in the Air Force 54

**5** Women on the March in the Army 74

**6** Women on the March in the Navy 92

**7** Women on the March in the Marine
 Corps 110

**8** Women on the March in the Coast Guard *126*

**9** Professional Opportunities in the Military
Health Fields *135*

**10** "Regardless of Race, Sex, Creed or
National Origin" *146*

Index *157*

# LIST OF
# ILLUSTRATIONS

| | |
|---|---|
| Brigadier General Elizabeth Hoisington | *13* |
| Revolutionary War heroine Molly Pitcher | *30* |
| Navy Yeomanettes during World War I | *36* |
| The first Waves to serve | *41* |
| Recruiters are the best source of information | *48* |
| A candidate takes the enlistment oath | *52* |
| Waf undergoing Air Force Security Police training | *57* |
| An Air Force Security Police trainee | *62* |
| An enlisted Waf aeromedical technician | *71* |
| An enlisted Wac aircraft controller | *78* |
| A Wac information specialist | *85* |
| One of the Army's military policewomen | *90* |
| A Wave crewmember aboard the *Sanctuary* | *95* |
| The first women chosen for Navy flight training | *103* |
| A woman marine sergeant serves as a commentator | *116* |
| This woman marine is a photographer | *123* |
| The Coast Guard's Officer Candidate School | *130* |
| A woman officer candidate trains aboard the *Unimak* | *132* |
| A Navy nurse in 1918 | *137* |
| One of the Army's nurse-midwives | *137* |
| Lieutenant Janette E. Baralli poses with a map | *148* |
| Lance Corporal Sally Ashland sets up a problem | *154* |

# 1

## A CEREMONY
## FOR
## PROMOTION

"The members of the press are cordially invited to attend the ceremony for promotion to Brigadier General of Colonel Anna Mae Hays, Chief of the Army Nurse Corps, and Colonel Elizabeth P. Hoisington, Director, Women's Army Corps. The ceremony will be held at 1000 hours, Thursday, 11 June 1970, in the Defense Audio-Visual Studio, Room 2E781, Pentagon, with the Secretary of the Army and Chief of Staff as hosts."

Well before 10 o'clock on June 11 reporters and friends of the two women who were to receive the silver stars of a brigadier general began to gather in Room 781 in the E, or outer, ring of the Pentagon's second floor. The room, normally used for press briefings, was not large, and soon filled up.

This was indeed a newsworthy occasion. For the first time in its 196-year history, the United States Army was promoting two women to the rank of brigadier general.

"Theirs was a long, slow path before receiving just recognition," said Army Chief of Staff General William C. Westmoreland during the promotion ceremony. The chief of staff helped pin silver stars to the new generals' shoulders and kissed each of them on the cheek. The kiss was "a new protocol for congratulating lady generals," he announced.

Secretary of the Army Stanley R. Resor, in his speech, called General Hays and General Hoisington "first ladies of the Army."

For Anna Mae Hays, promotion to the rank of brigadier general culminated a 28-year career as an Army nurse that began in 1942, shortly after her graduation with honors from the Allentown Hospital School of Nursing, in Pennsylvania. She had been out of school only a few months when the United States entered World War II. Hundreds of nurses were urgently needed to staff Army hospitals and clinics on military posts in the United States. Eventually, thousands of nurses would be needed as the Army grew in size and American soldiers went into combat in North Africa, Europe and the Pacific.

Anna Hays was among the first to respond to the Army's call for nurses. After receiving the gold bars of a second lieutenant, she reported to the Army hospital at Camp Claiborne, Louisiana, as an operating-room nurse. From Camp Claiborne she traveled halfway around the world to Lido, in northern India, for duty as an operating-room nurse with the U.S. Army's 20th General Hospital. Allied forces based in the Lido area were constructing an important supply road leading to China. The 20th General Hospital cared for the engineer battalions working on the road as well as combat troops, including Chinese soldiers, who were stationed at bases in eastern India.

After the war ended, Anna Hays spent five years at Army hospitals in the United States. She returned to overseas duty in 1950. The Korean conflict had begun and she was assigned as an operating-room supervisor at the 4th Field Hospital in South Korea. This was followed by several months in Japan, where she worked in the U.S. Army's big Tokyo hospital.

When she returned to the United States, Anna Hays moved into positions of increasing responsibility, for which she prepared by attending the Army's one-year nursing service administration course at Brooke Army Medical Center at Fort Sam Houston, Texas. In 1956, she was supervisor of the emergency room at Walter Reed General Hospital in Washington, D.C., when President Dwight D. Eisenhower was admitted for treatment for ileitus, an inflamation of the small intestine. Captain Hays was one of the president's nurses. Shortly thereafter, she left Walter Reed Hospital for a year of study at Columbia University, in New York City, where she earned a bachelor of science degree in nursing education.

While she studied at Columbia University, Anna Hays remained a member of the Army Nurse Corps, drawing her regular pay and allowances. After graduation, she continued to fill increasingly responsible supervisory or administrative positions in the Army nursing service.

In 1963, Anna Hays, by then a lieutenant colonel, moved to the Pentagon as assistant chief of the Army Nurse Corps. She left her post in the fall of 1966 to begin another year of study, this time at the Catholic University of America in Washington, D.C., where she earned a master of science degree in nursing. She returned to the Pentagon to take over as head of the Army Nurse Corps, a position that carried with it the rank of colonel, the highest military rank that could then be held by a woman in the United States Armed Forces.

Elizabeth P. Hoisington's military career began in November, 1942, when she enlisted in the recently organized Women's Army Auxiliary Corps, or WAAC, as it was generally known until its name was changed to Women's Army Corps (WAC) in 1943. Six months later she was commissioned a third officer (second lieutenant) at the Officer Candidate School, First WAAC Training Center, Fort Des Moines, Iowa.

The new officer was assigned to the WAAC Training Center at Fort Devens, Massachusetts, and then to a post in California. In April, 1944, she reported to Allied Commander Dwight Eisenhower's headquarters in London, England, as the executive officer of a WAC detachment. After the successful Allied invasion of France, she moved with General Eisenhower's headquarters to Paris and then to Frankfurt, Germany.

For several months after the defeat of Germany, Elizabeth Hoisington, by then a captain, remained on duty in Frankfurt with the American occupation forces. In 1946, however, the future director of the Women's Army Corps was one of the thousands of women who were released from duty with the WAC when the Army reduced its strength. Many of the women felt that their obligation to serve their country had

General William C. Westmoreland, Army Chief of Staff, and her mother pin silver stars to Brigadier General Elizabeth Hoisington's shoulders during the promotion ceremony in 1970 for the Army's first female general officers. *(U.S. Army)*

been discharged with the end of the war. But some of the former Wacs were convinced that they could continue to be of value to the Army and to the United States. Elizabeth Hoisington was in the latter group. When she was given the opportunity to return to temporary active duty in February, 1948, she readily agreed to do so. Later that year the Women's Armed Services Integration Act made it possible for women to have a permanent military career.

In addition to allowing women to serve in the Regular Air Force, the Regular Army, the Regular Navy and the Regular Marine Corps, the Integration Act gave servicewomen equal status with servicemen, with the exception that only men could be assigned to combat duty. Women were to receive the same privileges and benefits as men of corresponding grades, their chances of promotion were to be equal—within certain limitations—and they were to have an equal opportunity for training. However, the act limited the number of women permitted to hold some grades. And it limited the number of women who could become members of the Regular, as opposed to the Reserve, military establishment to 2 percent of the total strength of each of the services.

But even when women's Regular and Reserve numbers are combined, strength figures indicate that the services failed to reach the 2 percent figure. In 1949, a year after the Women's Armed Services Integration Act became law, the 9,277 women in the Army represented only 1.4 percent of that force. The Navy's 5,131 women constituted 1.1 percent of all naval personnel. In the Air Force 3,320 women made up 0.7 percent of the total strength and 353 women Marines represented 0.4 percent of the strength of that service.

Twenty years later the Army's 15,878 women made up 1 percent of its strength. The 8,636 women in the Navy were 1.1 percent of its total strength. In the Air Force 12,265 women were 1.4 percent of that service's strength. And 2,727 woman Marines were 0.8 percent of total Marine strength.

In spite of several praiseworthy provisions in the Integration Act, therefore, women found that equality with men in military training opportunities, assignments and promotions was by no means guaranteed.

For Captain Hoisington, return to active duty in the WAC meant an assignment to Tokyo as executive officer of the WAC battalion at the headquarters of the Army's Far East Command. This was followed by assignments that took her to Fort Monroe, Virginia; the Pentagon; the Presidio in San Francisco; the headquarters of the United States European Command in Paris; to the WAC Center at Fort McClellan, Alabama, as commanding officer; and in August, 1966, back to the Pentagon as Colonel Hoisington and director of the Women's Army Corps.

In 1970, when Colonel Hoisington and Colonel Hays were nominated for the rank of brigadier general, there were 41,405 women in the United States Armed Forces. The Army, with 16,724 women, had the most female members; the Air Force had 13,654 women on its rolls; the Navy had 8,609, and the Marine Corps had 2,418. For all of these women, the promotion to brigadier general of Elizabeth Hoisington and Anna Mae Hays represented a big step forward in their struggle to win full acceptance in what had always been considered a man's world.

In the past, the highest permanent grade that a woman officer could hope to achieve had been lieutenant colonel if she was a member of the Air Force, Army or Marines. In the Navy the equivalent grade was commander. Although the officers in charge of each service's Nurse Corps and women's branch could hold the rank of colonel, or captain in the case of the Navy, they held the higher grade only as long as they remained in that job. Upon their reassignment, they became lieutenant colonels or commanders again.

There were promotion restrictions in the lower officer grades as well. The Army's officer structure was typical. No more than 10 percent of all WAC officers could hold the rank of lieutenant colonel; between 19 and 31 percent could be majors; 23 to 25 percent could be captains; 18 to 30 percent could be first lieutenants; and another 18 to 30 percent could be second lieutenants. However, the combined percentages for the ranks of second lieutenant through major had to total 90 percent of the total WAC force.

Comparable figures for male officers were: lieutenant colonel—14 percent; major—19 percent; captain—23 percent; first lieutenant—18 percent; and second lieutenant—18 percent. The remainder were colonels and general officers.

And these were only some of the special restrictions that women faced. By law the number of women officers in the Regular Air Force and Regular Army had been limited to 2 percent of the total officer strength. Women officers in the Navy and the Marine Corps could number no more than 10 percent of the enlisted women in those services. Enlisted women in each of the services were limited to 2 percent of the total enlisted strength of that service. In addition to being restricted as to rank and numbers, many women officers were required to retire at an earlier age than their male counterparts.

Not all of the restrictions faced by women in uniform were a matter of law. Some resulted from the not yet discarded idea that the mission of the military woman was to free a man for combat duty. According to this way of thinking, a woman was in uniform, not because of her own special skills, but to act as a substitute for a man, who would then be freed to serve elsewhere. However, even as a substitute, a woman wasn't always welcome. Of her own experiences as a WAC officer during World War II, General Hoisington has written: "Forced to accept [women] by an act of Congress, the men had no choice but to grit their teeth—few smiled." And that attitude persisted in the years after the war.

Public Law 90–130, which President Lyndon B. Johnson signed on November 8, 1967, removed the ceiling on the grades that women officers could attain and made the rules for their separation or retirement from military service the same as those for men. The new law also removed the percentage limitations on the total number of women who could serve in the Air Force, Army, Navy and Marines. Public Law 90–130 didn't immediately solve all the problems of servicewomen, of course. But, as an official of the Defense Advisory Committee on Women in the Services put it: "The women now in military service are beginning to fade that image of a bench warmer and are becoming full and active members of the Armed Forces team."

The Armed Forces team of the United States is a large and many-faceted one. In 1973, 2,200,000 men and women were serving in the active military forces. Approximately 782,000 of them were in the Army; 674,000 were in the Air Force; 556,000 were in the Navy; and 189,000 were in the Marine Corps. In addition, the Department of Defense employed another one million people in a civilian capacity.

Heading the vast defense establishment is a secretary of defense, the principal adviser to the president on military matters. He is chosen by the president, but his appointment must be confirmed by the Senate.

Many people help the secretary of defense run his huge department. Some of them are assistant secretaries, who are in charge of such things as financial management, health and sanitation requirements, military property and supplies, intelligence activities, the Defense Department's relations with other countries, personnel management, public information and military communications.

All of the assistant secretaries are civilians, as are many of their staff members, but the secretary of defense has some military advisers. They are the Joint Chiefs of Staff, who also advise the president and the National Security Council. The chairman of the Joint Chiefs of Staff is the ranking military officer of the Armed Forces. Serving with him are the Air Force chief of staff, the Army chief of staff, the chief of Naval Operations and the commandant of the Marine Corps. They are chosen by the president from among the most competent officers of the four services.

In addition to their advisory duties, the Joint Chiefs of Staff supervise the activities of several military agencies that serve the entire Defense Department. These include the Defense Communications Agency, the Defense Intelligence Agency and the Defense Mapping Agency. The Joint Chiefs of Staff also control eight special combat forces that are organized according to their military function or the area in which they operate. In the former group are the Continental Air Defense Command, the Readiness Command and the Strategic Air Command. The latter group consists of the Alaskan Command, the Atlantic Command, the European Command, the Pacific Command and the Southern Command. These eight commands contain units from the four services.

Each member of the Joint Chiefs of Staff, other than the chairman, is the senior military officer of his service. However, the individual services are administered by civilian secretaries who are responsible to the secretary of defense. The Air Force is the youngest of the four armed services. It came into being as a separate organization in 1947. Before then, it was part of the Army and called the Army Air Forces. Earlier, it had been known as the Army Air Corps.

Today the Air Force has fifteen commands to carry out its official mission—to assist in preserving the peace and security of the United States. Three of the commands are combat commands with headquarters in the United States: the Aerospace Defense Command, which provides air defense for the United States; the Strategic Air Command, whose operating equipment includes long-range bombers and intercontinental missiles; and the Tactical Air Command, which supplies air support to ground forces. Four Air Force commands are based outside the United States: in Europe, the Pacific, Alaska and the Panama Canal Zone. The remaining commands are concerned with administration, supply, the development of new equipment, training programs, security matters, airlift and communications.

The United States Army can trace its history back to the troubled days before the Revolutionary War. In 1775, when conflict with Great Britain appeared inevitable, representatives of the thirteen American colonies, meeting in the Continental Congress, voted to raise ten divisions of infantry. They chose George Washington as their commander in chief. Assisted by militia forces raised by the colonies, the Continental army defeated the British to win the War for Independence.

With the coming of peace, the Continental army was reduced to a handful of men. In 1785, however, the new United

States Congress provided funds for a small Regular Army. In 1789, Congress established a Department of War, headed by a secretary of war, to administer both land and sea forces. A separate Navy Department was created nine years later.

In addition to fighting in its country's wars, the Army played an important part in opening the American West to settlement. The Army remained small, however, except when it was fighting a war. This remained the case until after World War II when unsettled world conditions required a large, well-equipped peacetime Army.

The present Department of the Army replaced the old Department of War in 1947. Its official mission is to provide support for the national and international policy and security of the United States.

Like the Air Force, the Army is divided into a number of commands. The Continental Army Command includes four armies based within the continental United States. The Materiel Command develops and provides weapons, munitions and other equipment for the Army. The Combat Development Command works out combat procedures for the Army to use if it should have to fight a war. The Army's extensive communications systems are the responsibility of the Strategic Communications Command. The Recruiting Command supplies men and women for the Army. The Army also has an Intelligence Command to handle security matters and a Criminal Investigation Command.

The Army has forces based in Europe, the Pacific area, Alaska and the Canal Zone, and forces assigned to the Air Defense and Readiness Commands that operate with units from other services, under the direction of the Joint Chiefs of Staff.

The United States Navy, whose mission is to protect the country by the effective prosecution of war at sea, began as a small naval force during the Revolutionary War. That force was disbanded when the war ended, to be revived again in 1794. The Department of the Navy was established in 1798 to conduct the naval affairs of the United States.

During the nineteenth century the Navy exchanged its sailing ships for steam-powered vessels. Steel hulls replaced wooden hulls. The mighty battleship had made an appearance by 1890, inaugurating a period of rapid naval expansion for the United States. Along with its battleships, the U.S. Navy made effective use of destroyers during World War I. Destroyers saw action again in World War II, but the aircraft carrier replaced the battleship as a major naval vessel. The Navy's submarines also played an important role in the Allied victory in World War II. At the end of that war the United States Navy was the most powerful naval force in the world.

Today, the Navy's major commands afloat are the Pacific Fleet; the Atlantic Fleet; the Naval Forces, Europe; and the Military Sealift Command. Only a small portion of the Navy's personnel is at sea at any one time, however. A great many people are needed at shore stations to support the seagoing forces. They are engaged in such activities as personnel management, providing supplies, developing new weapons, ships, aircraft and other equipment, handling communications and training Navy men and women.

The United States Marine Corps operates as a separate service within the Department of the Navy. While the commandant of the Marine Corps is a member of the Joint Chiefs of Staff, his participation is limited to matters that involve the Corps.

Since its establishment in 1775 by the Continental Congress, the Marine Corps has acted as a force-in-readiness, prepared to deploy on short notice to any part of the world. Its primary mission is to provide forces for the seizure and defense of advanced naval bases and to conduct land operations in support of naval campaigns. The Corps also provides security forces for naval bases and for American embassies throughout the world. In addition, the Marine Corps is charged with performing "such other duties as the President might require."

The largest Marine Corps force, with two infantry divisions and two aircraft wings, plus supporting units, is the Fleet Marine Force, Pacific. The Fleet Marine Force, Atlantic, with one division and one aircraft wing, plus supporting units, has headquarters on the United States east coast. In addition to its two combat forces, the Marine Corps has a unit that recruits and trains marines, one that provides them with supplies and equipment and another that maintains Marine installations.

Although it normally operates as a service within the Department of Transportation, the United States Coast Guard is also a branch of the Armed Forces. In time of war, or when the president directs, the Coast Guard becomes a part of the Navy. Indeed, the Coast Guard, called the Revenue Marine until 1915, was the nation's only seagoing force until the Navy was formed.

Congress established what is now the Coast Guard in 1790 as a maritime law enforcement agency. It still enforces federal laws on the high seas and on the navigable waters of the United States. But the Coast Guard has many other duties. It is charged with protecting life and property in and around the navigable waters of the United States and it enforces regulations aimed at preventing the pollution of those waters. It administers merchant marine and boating safety programs. Coast guardsmen on ocean stations in the North Atlantic and the Pacific supply meteorological information to ships, aircraft and the National Weather Service. They also perform search and rescue missions, collect oceanographic data and furnish navigation information to ships and aircraft.

Coast Guard navigation aids, such as lightships, buoys, fog signals and long-range electronic aids (loran), guide ships and aircraft in the navigable waters of the United States, and in many other parts of the world as well. The Coast Guard is responsible for the security of United States ports and it provides icebreaking services when they are required by domestic commerce or military operations.

Along with its other missions the Coast Guard maintains a state of readiness to function as a specialized service in the Navy. Its uniformed personnel, whose rank and pay structure is the same as that of members of the Navy, have fought alongside United States naval forces in every one of the country's wars.

# 2

## SOME WOMEN
## WHO
## WENT TO WAR

Women soldiers are by no means unknown in history, although very few of them achieved positions of command. Legends of ancient Greece tell of the exploits of women warriors who were called Amazons. The home of the Amazons is difficult to pinpoint, but they are said to have fought battles with the Phrygians, the Lycians, the Atticans and other ancient peoples.

Statues of the Amazons show them carrying crescent-shaped shields, bows, spears and light double axes as weapons. Sometimes the women warriors are depicted wearing a thin dress caught up at the waist to allow freedom of movement. Other sculptors have portrayed them in close-fitting trousers and high caps.

Legends of women warriors abound in Africa where they

are credited with founding cities, leading migrations and conquering kingdoms. The women warriors of Dahomey, in western Africa, were more than a legend, however. During the middle years of the nineteenth century they constituted a formidable fighting force that won many battles.

King Afadja of Dahomey began the training of women as soldiers and they soon proved to be better fighters than their male counterparts. Only the finest girls of Dahomey were recruited for the army. Their arduous training included forced long-distance marches, wrestling and combat with spears. There was also racing over an obstacle course obstructed by a fifteen-foot-high, six-foot-wide barrier of thorns and a ditch full of burning and smoldering wood.

Dahomey's women warriors were honored by their fellow citizens and they enjoyed a high standard of living. King Gezo of Dahomey, who reigned between 1818 and 1858, considered them to be his best soldiers. He called the women "the flower of my force."

In battle the women warriors fought in regiments of their own, each with its distinctive uniform and badges. For weapons they used blunderbusses, flint muskets, and bows and arrows. Surprise was one of their most successful tactics. Avoiding the main routes of travel and maintaining strict silence, the warriors would surround an unsuspecting town and attack just before dawn. Usually an attack achieved its objective but, if it failed, the women soldiers were expected to fight to the last.

British history records the story of a famous woman warrior who challenged the Roman invaders of her country. She was Boadicea, queen of the Iceni tribe, who, in A.D. 60, led her people in a revolt against Roman rule. Queen Boadicea and her followers rode into battle in chariots with sharp scythes fixed to the axle trees. They killed many Roman soldiers and burned several Roman settlements. But in a final desperate battle the Iceni were defeated. Boadicea either took poison or died of shock in A.D. 62. Her efforts were not in vain, however, because after the uprising the Romans adopted a more lenient policy toward the Iceni.

France produced the most famous of all women soldiers —Joan of Arc. Joan, who was born in 1412, grew up at a time when the English controlled much of northern and western France. During this period, the kings of England claimed that they were also the rulers of France.

Joan of Arc was a deeply religious girl who maintained that she heard voices directing her to help the French dauphin, Charles VII, establish himself as the rightful king of France. Joan was still in her teens when she left Domrémy, her native village, to persuade Charles that she should be allowed to take part in a military action against the English who were attacking Orléans in north-central France. Her arguments were so convincing that Charles and his initially sceptical advisers finally gave her permission to go to Orléans.

No authentic portrait of Joan of Arc has ever been found, but she is reported to have been an attractive girl with a bright, smiling face who wore her hair cut short like a soldier's. She liked fine clothes and good horses.

At Orléans Joan rode into battle on a handsome black horse. She wore a suit of white armor and carried a lance, a consecrated sword and a banner that carried the motto "Jésu Maria."

Inspired by Joan of Arc, the French army drove the English from besieged Orléans. Joan was in the thick of the fighting. During one of the engagements she was wounded in the shoulder by an enemy arrow while placing the first scaling ladder against the wall of the English-held fort. But, as soon as the shock of the wound wore off, she returned to lead another assault on the fort, which was captured.

The French success at Orléans was followed by other victories in which Joan played a leading role. Within two months, she had made it possible for Charles VII to be proclaimed king of France. The ceremony, which Joan attended, took place in July, 1429.

Paris, the capital, was still held by the English, however, and Joan wished to make the French victory complete by taking that city. Unfortunately, her attempt to enter Paris at the head of the king's forces failed. During the fighting Joan suffered a wound in the thigh. Although the wound was severe, she refused to leave the battlefield. Her fellow soldiers, concerned for their leader's safety, finally had to drag her away.

After some weeks of inactivity, Joan of Arc resumed her military career. By the spring of 1430 she had fought her way to Compiègne, a fortress town that she had captured the previous year. Compiègne was under attack by the Burgundian allies of the English and Joan planned to help the townspeople repulse the besiegers. Shortly after her arrival she led an attack against the Burgundians. In the ensuing fight, her forces were driven back into the town and Joan was captured as she charged the enemy in an attempt to save her comrades.

The Burgundians sold their prize captive to the English, who were anxious to end her influence over the people of

France. After a lengthy trial the French heroine was condemned to death and burned alive at Rouen on May 30, 1431. Although Joan of Arc's religious inspiration played an important part in her acceptance as a woman soldier, she also displayed considerable ability as a military leader. Far from being an honorary commander of Charles VII's forces, she planned campaigns and took an active part in carrying them out, often at great risk to herself.

Accounts of the Revolutionary War, the War of 1812 and the Civil War indicate that a few American women managed to serve as soldiers even though their presence on the battlefield was unauthorized. However, unlike Joan of Arc who led the forces of Charles VII as a woman, most of America's pioneer women soldiers had to masquerade as men. There are no official accounts of their activities, but in some cases the women later wrote about their experiences.

Deborah Sampson, who fought in the Revolutionary War, was one of the first of these pioneers. Deborah wanted to take an active part in the colonies' struggle for independence. Because women were not accepted in any of the colonial forces, she decided to enlist as a man. The enterprising Deborah arranged her hair in a masculine style and donned a suit of men's clothing. Thus disguised, she was able to join the 4th Massachusetts Regiment, using the name Robert Shurtleff.

Fortunately, Deborah Sampson was a strong woman who was used to hard work and outdoor life. In the 4th Massachusetts she had to endure long marches and primitive living conditions. Nevertheless, for three years she managed to keep up with her male counterparts. During that period she was wounded three times, but the wounds were too slight to require treatment that would reveal Robert Shurtleff to be a woman.

In the fall of 1781, during the Yorktown campaign that brought the Revolutionary War to a close, Deborah came down with what was diagnosed as brain fever, a form of meningitis. This was a serious illness that required hospitalization and, at the hospital, Deborah's secret was discovered. She was not discharged from the army immediately, however. When the impostor regained her health, she was ordered to report to George Washington's headquarters. She carried a letter for the general explaining what she had done. Washington is said to have read the letter in silence. Then, without saying a single word to Deborah, he handed her a set of discharge papers and her mustering-out pay.

Deborah Sampson later wrote about her experiences in the army, describing several hazardous missions that she carried out as successfully as any male soldier could have done.

Another heroine of the Revolutionary War, Mary Hays, or Molly Pitcher, as she came to be called, attached herself to the 7th Pennsylvania Regiment. Her husband, John Hays, was an artilleryman in that regiment and, like many other soldiers' wives, Molly wanted to be near her husband. Military authorities did not encourage wives to accompany their soldier husbands into combat areas, but it was recognized that the women performed many useful services, such as looking after the sick and wounded, washing clothes and cooking. Molly probably received the name Molly Pitcher because she carried water to thirsty soldiers.

Revolutionary War heroine Molly Pitcher is depicted ramming a charge into her husband's gun in a lithograph by Currier and Ives. *(Library of Congress)*

But Molly did more to help the American cause than carry water. On a hot June day, in 1778, at Monmouth Courthouse, New Jersey, the Americans attacked a British force that was moving overland from Philadelphia to New York City. It was the colonials' first major offensive after a difficult winter spent at Valley Forge, Pennsylvania. In spite of the hardships they endured at Valley Forge, General George Washington's men had trained throughout the winter, and they posed a serious threat to the British.

In the fighting that raged all day long at Monmouth Courthouse John Hays served as a gunner for the Americans. Molly, as she had done many times before, carried water to the soldiers. Both husband and wife were in great danger from heavy British gunfire.

According to some accounts of the battle, Molly noticed that her husband's gun had fallen silent. When she reached the gun emplacement, she found that the members of the crew had all been wounded by an exploding British shell. After helping the men to a safe place, Molly returned to the gun. She swabbed it out, rammed home a charge and fired, putting a badly needed gun back into service for the Americans.

Eventually a replacement crew arrived to take over the gun, but Molly's help was still needed. She remained on duty as a rammer until another rammer could be found. Then she returned to caring for the wounded, including her own husband, and bringing water to the soldiers.

The sight of Molly, ragged and begrimed, helping to keep her husband's gun in action, is said to have inspired the Americans to renew their efforts to defeat the British. Although they failed to win a decisive victory, the colonials forced the redcoats to withdraw to New York. Moreover, the British never regained the offensive in the New Jersey area.

When General Washington heard of Molly's part in the battle of Monmouth Courthouse, he thanked her personally. She became known as "Captain Molly" and after the war lived for many years at Carlisle Barracks in Pennsylvania. A figure representing Captain Molly appears on a bas-relief at the base of the memorial on the site of the Monmouth battlefield.

The War of 1812 produced at least one service woman. She was Lucy Brewer, who joined the Marines under the name of George Baker. In order to enlist as a young man, Lucy cut her hair, dressed in men's clothing and spoke in the deepest voice she could manage. Her deception was made easier by the wide, baggy trousers and loose blouse and jacket worn by the marines of that day.

Early in her military career Lucy served on the *Constitution,* the 44-gun frigate that became famous as "Old Ironsides." She took part in the *Constitution*'s heroic victory over the British 38-gun frigate *Guerrière.* The *Constitution* also defeated the British frigate *Java* in another important battle.

Somehow Lucy managed to escape detection during her three years as a marine. After her discharge she described her experiences in a book entitled *The Female Marine.* It was a popular book, but many readers doubted its authenticity, partly because Lucy had used the pseudonym Louisa Baker when she wrote the book. Lucy subsequently published another edition using her own name.

During the Civil War both the Union and the Confederate forces had a few women in their ranks. In most cases they found it necessary to disguise themselves as men.

Probably the most flamboyant of the women who served in the Civil War was Loreta Velasquez, who joined the Confederate Army as Henry Buford. Her disguise included a false mustache and chin whiskers.

In 1861, Loreta, posing as Henry Buford, raised a troop of soldiers to fight for the Confederacy. In return, "Henry Buford" was commissioned a lieutenant and placed in command of the group.

As the leader of soldiers that she had enlisted herself, Loreta enjoyed a great deal of freedom. She was at Bull Run, in northern Virginia, when the Confederate forces won the first big battle of the Civil War. After Bull Run Loreta undertook an espionage mission for which, according to her own account, she adopted the disguise of a countrywoman's calico dress, woolen shawl, sunbonnet and rough shoes. In this attire Loreta crossed the Union lines and reached Washington. Two weeks later she returned to the Confederate headquarters with information about the North's plans to win control of the Mississippi River. That information had already been obtained from other sources, however, and a disenchanted Loreta decided to return to the battlefield.

Early in 1862 "Lieutenant Buford" appeared in Tennessee where "he" took part in the unsuccessful defense of Fort Donelson. Seventeen thousand Confederate soldiers were captured at Fort Donelson, but Loreta was among the 4,000 that managed to escape. Shortly afterward she was shot in the foot, a wound that required several weeks of recuperation in New Orleans.

During her stay in New Orleans, Loreta aroused the suspicions of Confederate officials who suspected that "Lieutenant Buford" might be a Union spy. Loreta talked her way out of that accusation only to be charged with masquerading as a Confederate officer. Loreta had to admit that the charge was true. She was Loreta Velasquez, not Lieutenant Henry Buford. Loreta asked to be allowed to continue in the Confederate Army, but her request was denied. Instead, she was sentenced to ten days in jail and ordered to pay a small fine. The exposure of her masquerade failed to discourage Loreta. Before long she was back in a Confederate uniform, this time as an infantryman. But Loreta missed the freedom she had had as an officer. Resuming the identity of Lieutenant Buford, she applied for a post as a cavalry officer in the Army of East Tennessee. Cavalry officers were needed and "Lieutenant Buford's" application was accepted.

When Loreta, in the uniform of a Confederate cavalry officer, reported for duty, she was assigned the dangerous task of leading scouting patrols into the disputed area between the opposing armies. Occasionally, she scouted enemy-held territory as well. During one of her patrols Loreta was hit in the shoulder and arm by artillery fire. Although she was able to remount her horse and lead her men twenty miles to safety, the wounds were serious enough to require hospitalization. Loreta managed to maintain her masquerade until she was placed aboard a hospital train. Then "Lieutenant Buford's" true identity was discovered once again, but the impostor escaped punishment.

When Loreta recovered from her wounds she made no further attempts to take an active part in the fighting. However, she continued to help the Confederate cause as an espionage agent.

During the Civil War several thousand women served with the Union and Confederate forces as nurses, but they served as civilians. Union nurses, who were organized into a Nurse Corps, received $12 a month, one ration a day and lodgings. To be hired as a nurse, a woman had to be over 30 years of age and she had to wear a brown or black dress while on duty. Four Civil War nurses worked on the steamer *Red Rover* which served as a Union hospital ship.

Civilian nurses were hired again during the Spanish-American War in 1898. They took care of sick and wounded soldiers and sailors in the United States, the Philippines, Cuba, Puerto Rico and aboard troop ships.

The Civil War and the Spanish-American War demonstrated the need for a permanently organized military nursing service. It was not until 1901, however, that the Army established its Nurse Corps. The Navy Nurse Corps came into being in 1908. Although the women who were accepted for nursing duty were part of the Army and the Navy, they were not given military rank, nor did they receive pay or benefits equal to those received by male members of the Armed Forces. It was 1944 before military nurses achieved even partial equality with servicemen.

In the meantime, the Armed Forces of the United States had fought in World War I, a conflict that placed a severe strain on the nation's available manpower. Early in the war, the commander in chief of the American Expeditionary Forces, General John J. Pershing, suggested that a hundred women be enlisted in the Army, trained and sent to France as badly needed French-speaking telephone operators. General Pershing was familiar with the service groups, called auxiliaries, that the British had organized for women. Uniformed members of the auxiliaries performed a number of noncombat duties, effectively increasing the strength of the British military forces.

Unfortunately, United States Army regulations would not allow an American version of the uniformed British auxilia-

Navy Yeomanettes pose with a sailor during World War I. *(National Archives)*

ries. General Pershing got his telephone operators, but they were civilians who worked for the Army under contract.

The United States Navy, on the other hand, with regulations that referred to "yeomen," but failed to specify that they must be males, decided that it could enroll women. And women were anxious to sign up. Approximately 13,000 of them enlisted as Navy "Yeomanettes" and Marine Corps "Marinettes."

Unlike the members of the Army and Navy Nurse Corps, the Yeomanettes and Marinettes were given full military status. Moreover, they received the same pay and benefits as males of the same rank. Yeomanettes and Marinettes, serving as clerks, stenographers, typists and telephone operators, freed thousands of males for combat and sea duty. The Marinettes, whose recruiting slogan was "Free a Marine to Fight," began each day with close order drill. The women became so proficient that they took part in many parades and ceremonies.

Once the war was over, however, there was no further need for the services of the Yeomanettes and Marinettes. Both organizations were disbanded in 1919. With the exception of the women serving in the Army and Navy Nurse Corps, the Armed Forces of the United States reverted to their former all-male status.

Because the Yeomanettes and Marinettes had made valuable contributions to the war effort, interest in the possibility of using women in the Armed Forces carried over into the immediate postwar years. Several women's organizations backed the idea as part of a drive for women's rights. Miss Anita Phipps, the Army's director of women's relations, proposed that the Army establish a women's service corps. Army Major Everett S. Hughes, who conducted a two-year study of the feasibility of opening the Army to women, went a step further. He recommended that women be fully integrated into the Army. Nothing came of either proposal.

During the 1930s the United States Army and Navy were small organizations that needed women's services only as nurses, and not many of them were required. In the years between World War I and World War II the combined strength of the Army and the Navy Nurse Corps averaged about 1,500.

The possibility of accepting women for service in the Armed Forces was discussed again when World War II began in Europe and it appeared that the United States might become involved. In 1941 Congresswoman Edith N. Rogers sponsored a bill establishing a Woman's Auxiliary Army Corps for Service with the Army (WAAC). Initially, most Army officials opposed Mrs. Rogers' bill even though it authorized women to serve *with,* rather than *in,* the Army.

The Japanese attack on Pearl Harbor (on December 7, 1941) and the entry of the United States into World War II curtailed what otherwise would have been a lengthy debate on the WAAC bill. Spurred by the urgent need to increase the country's military strength, Congress passed the bill and it was signed into law by President Franklin D. Roosevelt on May 14, 1942. A short time later the president signed another bill creating the Women's Reserve of the Navy, or WAVES (Women Accepted for Volunteer Emergency Service).

Unlike the women who joined the WAAC, Waves were authorized to serve *in* the Navy. Being in the Navy meant that they were entitled to military benefits, such as free mailing, government insurance, allotments to dependents, reinstatement rights to jobs and veterans' bonuses, none of which were available to Waacs. Women marines enjoyed a status similar to that of the Waves after the Marine Corps Women's Reserve was activated in February, 1943.

During World War II the Coast Guard functioned as part of the Navy. The Coast Guard's Women's Reserve was organized in November, 1942, and its members were called Spars. The name derives from an abbreviation of the Coast Guard motto, *Semper Paratus,* and its English translation, Always Ready.

The Army's women gained full military status in 1943 when the Women's Auxiliary Army Corps became the

Women's Army Corps (WAC), a branch of the Army. Women had proven to be highly efficient replacements for men, and the Army made the change to improve administration and to encourage recruitment.

All of the services soon found that women could be used in many more jobs than the mainly clerical ones allotted to them. Before the first Waacs had completed their training, plans to expand the Corps from the original 25,000 limit on enrollment were under consideration. The ceiling was eventually set at 200,000. Actual strength, however, never exceeded 100,000.

Waacs, and later, Wacs, were assigned to the Army Air Forces, the Army Service Forces and the Army Ground Forces. They served in almost all overseas areas where Army troops were stationed and at most Army posts in the United States. With the exception of combat-related specialties, virtually no military occupation remained closed to them.

Wacs assigned to the Army Air Forces had perhaps the widest range of job opportunities. They received assignments as weather forecasters, Link-trainer instructors, airplane mechanics, control tower operators, electrical and radio specialists, sheet-metal workers, bombsight maintenance specialists, photolaboratory technicians, photo interpreters, cryptographers and parachute riggers, to name just a few of the posts that they occupied. By January of 1945, more than 200 different job categories were filled by enlisted Air Wacs. Wac officers held more than 60 different types of jobs.

The Army Service Forces utilized women in such varied jobs as telephone and teletypewriter operators, cryptanalysts, medical technicians, postal clerks and transportation experts. Women also worked on the supersecret nuclear bomb project.

Wacs served on the staffs of the Army Ground Forces' many training schools and a large WAC unit processed troops for overseas replacements.

Overseas assignments began for Wacs in December, 1942. They were eventually sent to every corner of the globe, with the largest number going to Europe. At their overseas posts the women presented no special health, morale or disciplinary problems despite weather conditions, housing and food that often left much to be desired. Their attrition rate was about the same as the rate for noncombat men.

Like their sisters in the WAC, the women who enlisted in the WAVES served in a variety of positions. They worked as airplane mechanics, parachute packers, Link-trainer instructors, gunnery instructors, air traffic controllers, storekeepers, personnel specialists, secretaries, typists, and as occupational and physical therapy assistants. Some WAVE officers were assigned to naval air crews as navigators, and, in limited numbers, they served in the Medical Service and Dental Corps.

Waves did not receive assignments outside the continental United States until September, 1944, but at home they were eagerly sought after for duty at naval hospitals, air stations, supply depots and naval yards. They accounted for as many as 55 percent of the Navy Department's uniformed personnel stationed in Washington, D.C. The WAVES reached a peak strength of 86,000 in 1945 when 13 percent of all shore-based naval personnel in the United States were women.

At their peak World War II strength Women Marines

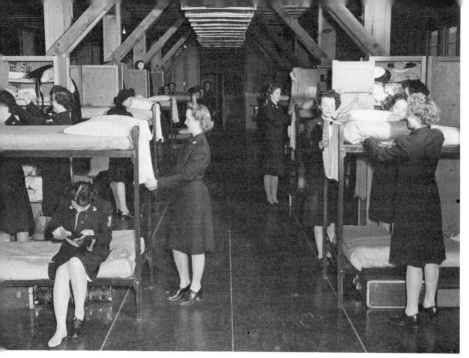

The first Waves to serve outside the continental United States during World War II settle into their quarters at Pearl Harbor in Hawaii. (U.S. Navy)

numbered 18,409. The lady leathernecks served in over 200 different kinds of jobs, among them traffic controller, photographer, artist, parachute rigger, truck driver, cook, stenographer and clerk.

Approximately 11,000 women joined the SPARS during World War II to take over administrative and clerical duties at Coast Guard shore stations. SPAR officers, who received their training at the Coast Guard Academy at New London, Connecticut, were the first women to attend a military academy. Upon completion of their training, they took over posts in communications, finance, supply, personnel, training, procurement, intelligence and law.

Enlisted Spars were assigned as stenographers, storekeepers, hospital corpsmen, radio technicians, loran operators, photographers, chaplain's assistants, draftsmen, parachute riggers, tailors and drivers.

In the early years of the war a special group of women ferried planes for the Army Air Forces, but they flew as civilian, rather than military, aviators. The women pilots, who were known as Wasps (Women Airforce Service Pilots), received much the same training as male aviation cadets and their elimination rates compared favorably with the washout rates for male cadets. The women received no gunnery training, however, and only limited training in formation flying and aerobatics.

Ferrying was the principal duty assigned to the Wasps, but they also performed tracking and searchlight missions, simulated bombing missions, radio control work, instrument instruction and administrative flying.

Male pilots were inclined to resent the presence of the Wasps who sometimes were qualified to fly planes that the men had not yet learned to handle. Resentment very often turned to admiration, however, because most of the Wasps did an excellent job.

Late in 1944, a growing surplus of male pilots reduced the need for the services of women flyers and the WASP was deactivated. When the program came to an end, the WASP had 916 women on its rolls.

During World War II approximately 350,000 women served with the WAC, WAVES, Women Marines, SPARS, the Army Nurse Corps and the Navy Nurse Corps. They made up about 3 percent of a total of 12 million persons who served in the United States Armed Forces. On the whole, these thousands of women performed in an outstanding manner. Moreover, they quickly demonstrated that they could handle many different kinds of jobs. The list of positions open to women expanded steadily during the war as did the specialist training programs available to them.

While some women did receive responsible and interesting technical or professional assignments during their World War II military service, a great many more were assigned to the same kinds of clerical and administrative positions that women traditionally filled in civilian life. Approximately half of the enlisted women in the WAC held such positions. In the other women's services, the highest concentration of assignments was also in the clerical and administrative fields.

Nevertheless, most women were satisfied with their World War II military service. In a study conducted in Europe shortly before the end of the war, 90 percent of the WAC officers and 65 percent of the enlisted women questioned said they would join the WAC again. Moreover, 69 percent of the officers and 37 percent of the enlisted women indicated that they might be interested in remaining in the WAC after the war.

Within a year after the end of the war, however, the majority of Wacs, Waves, and Women Marines had been discharged or placed on inactive duty. The SPARS were disbanded. But the women had successfully demonstrated their value to their country's military forces. In 1948 the Women's Armed Services Integration Act made it possible for them to join the Regular Air Force, Army, Navy and Marine Corps. In the meantime, the Army-Navy Nurse Act of 1947 had established the Army Nurse Corps, the Navy Nurse Corps and the services' other medical corps, as permanent components of the Army and the Navy. These are the laws that opened the door to military careers for today's women.

# 3

## A CHOICE
## WORTH CONSIDERING

Although the Women's Armed Services Integration Act and the Army-Navy Nurse Act opened the door to women who wanted a career in the armed services, not many were interested. During the 1950s and 1960s the number of women in uniform amounted to little more than 1 percent of the total force. Even during the Korean conflict, the percentage of women did not exceed 1.3 percent. In 1972 it reached 1.9 percent, still a very small portion of the country's military strength.

By 1972, however, the Defense Department was engaged in a review of its policies toward women. The women's rights movement had focused attention on restricted assignments which limited career opportunities for military women, and on regulations which discriminated against them. Moreover, the advent of the All-Volunteer Force made it imperative that the armed services make more effective utilization of their women members. The All-Volunteer Force meant that the services would be relying on volunteers alone to fill their ranks. It also meant fewer men would be volunteering as an alternative to being drafted. But women, who had always been volunteers, could take over many military jobs if they were given the opportunity and training to do so. The Department of Defense decided that women, and other minority groups, should have that opportunity.

The Defense Department's determination to make military service a model of equal opportunity is expressed in a Department statement entitled "Human Goals." The statement says in part: "Our Nation was founded on the Principle that the Individual has infinite dignity and worth. The Department of Defense, which exists to keep the Nation secure and at peace, must always be guided by this Principle. In all that we do, we must show respect for the Serviceman, the Servicewoman and the Civilian Employee, recognizing their individual needs, aspirations and capabilities.

"The defense of the Nation requires a well-trained force, Military and Civilian, Regular and Reserve. To provide such a force we must increase the attractiveness of a career in Defense so that the Service member and the Civilian employee will feel the highest pride in themselves and their work, in the uniform and the military profession.

"The attainment of these goals requires that we strive:

•To attract to the Defense Service people with ability, dedication and capacity for growth.
•To provide opportunity for everyone, Military and Civilian, to rise to as high a level of responsibility as possible,

dependent only on individual talent and diligence.

•To make Military and Civilian service in the Department of Defense a model of equal opportunity for all regardless of race, sex, creed, or national origin, and to hold those who do business with the Department of Defense to full compliance with the policy of equal employment opportunity."

Nowhere are opportunities for women increasing faster than in the Armed Forces. Moreover, the Air Force, the Army, the Navy and, to a lesser extent, the Marines, are actively seeking to enroll more women. The number of women in uniform is expected to reach 130,000 in 1978, more than twice the number of servicewomen on the rolls in 1974.

The woman who does decide to don the uniform of one of the armed services will find a wide variety of occupations open to her. Her pay and other benefits will be the same as those received by men of the same grade. And, with few exceptions, she will be considered for training and assignments on the same basis as her male counterparts.

Asked why she joined the Army, an eighteen-year-old recruit said: "I joined for the school, the education, and the benefits, and also, I just wanted to change my life. I hadn't been doing anything."

Recruit Judy Board joined the Army to become a military policewoman. "Why an MP? Because I was already into computers and to go into police work, I would have had to go back to school again. Here, I can go ahead and go through school [for military police training], be an MP, and then go ahead and get a degree."

Information about career opportunities for women in the

Recruiters are the best source of current information on the jobs and training opportunities that are currently available in the services they represent. Here, a prospective enlistee talks with an Air Force recruiter. *(Gene Gurney)*

Armed Forces can be obtained from Air Force, Army, Navy, Marine Corps and Coast Guard recruiters located at recruiting offices throughout the United States. The recruiter's job is to help young people find a rewarding career, and at the same time provide the armed services with the capable and dedicated members that they must have if the country is to remain strong. The recruiter does not pressure anyone into signing up, but he will outline the advantages of the service he represents and supply reliable information about requirements for enlistment or commissioning, military occupations, training opportunities, pay and other benefits of military service. In some cases the recruiter will be a woman member of the Armed Forces who can provide firsthand information of the opportunities available to women in her service.

If it is not convenient to visit a recruiter, the young woman who is seeking information about a military career can write to the offices in charge of recruiting for each of the military services. She will receive a selection of printed material designed to answer most, if not all, of her questions.*

*For information about Air Force careers for enlisted women write to:

Air Force Opportunities
Box A
Randolph Air Force Base, Texas 78148

For information about careers for women Air Force officers write to:

USAF Recruiting Service (RSAV)
Randolph Air Force Base, Texas 78148

For information about enlisted and officer careers in the Women's Army Corps write to:

Headquarters, U.S. Army Recruiting Command
Fort Sheridan, Illinois 60037

For information about Navy careers for enlisted women write to:

Navy Opportunity Information Center
P.O. Box 2000
Pelham Manor, New York 10803

For information about Navy careers for women officers write to:

Department of the Navy
Navy Recruiting Command
4015 Wilson Blvd.
Arlington, Virginia 22203

For information about enlisted and officer careers for women in the Marine Corps write to:

Headquarters, U.S. Marine Corps
Washington, D.C. 20380

For information about enlisted and officer careers for women in the Coast Guard write to:

Commandant, (PTP-2)
U.S. Coast Guard
Washington, D.C. 20590

Young women who are investigating the possibilities of a military career will find that enlistment and commissioning requirements vary only slightly among the services. All require women enlistees to have a high school diploma or its equivalent. The woman who wishes to enter military service as a commissioned officer must have a college degree. Applicants are also required to meet the mental and physical standards for enlistment or commissioning.

Her talks with recruiters and study of brochures obtained from the services will provide a prospective enlistee with information about the many occupations that are open to qualified women who join the Air Force, the Army, the Navy, the Marine Corps or the Coast Guard. Recruiters are eager to discuss military career fields. Moreover, recruiters can administer a series of aptitude tests to determine if a candidate has the ability to succeed in the job she thinks she wants. The tests will also indicate in what other career fields she would be successful. In some cases a recruiter can guarantee that a qualified enlistee will be assigned to the job of her choice. If that is not possible, the recruiter may be able to arrange for her to be assigned within the general vocational field of her choice.

Armed with the information that she has acquired about enlistment requirements, career opportunities and other aspects of military life, a young woman is ready to make important decisions. The first thing she must decide is whether or not she wants to embark on a military career. If she decides that she does, she must choose from among the services. Should she enlist in the Air Force, the Army, the Navy, the

Marine Corps or the Coast Guard? She will have learned that each service has advantages and disadvantages and the choice may not be an easy one.

After a prospective enlistee has decided which service she wishes to join, the next step is another visit to that service's recruiting office. This time she will take a short mental exam. If she passes, she will be asked to fill out a formal application for enlistment. She will also be told when to report to the nearest Armed Forces Examining and Entrance Station for a day of more written tests, interviews and a complete physical examination. Her travel expenses will be paid by the government. Usually, candidates learn on the testing day whether or not they will be accepted for enlistment.

For those who are accepted, there is a choice of enlistment dates. Some wish to report immediately. Others prefer to wait from 30 to 60 days. On the agreed-upon date the prospective enlistee reports back to the Armed Forces Examining and Entrance Station. She may have to undergo a brief recheck if her physical examination took place more than ten days previously. If all her records are in order, she takes the oath of enlistment. The oath contains a statement that she "voluntarily enlisted under the conditions prescribed by law" and gives the number of years for which she has agreed to enlist. It continues: "I do solemnly swear (or affirm) that I will support and defend the Constitution of the United States against all enemies, foreign and domestic; that I will bear true faith and allegiance to the same; and that I will obey the orders of the President of the United States and the orders of the officers appointed over me, according to regula-

With her right hand raised, a candidate for the Marine Corps' officer training course takes the enlistment oath. *(U.S. Marine Corps)*

tions, and the Uniform Code of Military Justice. So help me God."

After taking the oath, the enlistee is a member of the Armed Forces of the United States. Arrangements have already been made for her travel to a basic training center. Within hours, she is on her way.

A prospective officer candidate, who has completed her college work, or is about to complete it, can make arrangements to join the service of her choice through one of that service's recruiting offices. As part of her application for officer training, a candidate must pass an officer qualifying test and a physical examination. Interviews, letters of recommendation and a security check are also required. Because standards are high, the successful applicant is a member of a select group. After being sworn in as an officer candidate, she reports to her service's officer training center to begin her preparation for an exciting military career.

# 4

## WOMEN ON
## THE MARCH
## IN THE AIR FORCE

The United States Air Force begins the training of its young women recruits at Lackland Air Force Base near San Antonio, Texas. Both men and women receive their basic training at Lackland, the "Gateway to the Air Force."

When she arrives at San Antonio, a new Waf (derived from Women in the Air Force) will be met by an Air Force guide who will take her, and probably several other recruits, to Lackland's personnel processing center where the newcomers will be assigned to a training flight. A "flight" is the Air Force's basic unit. For six weeks the recruit will train with the 50 or 60 other new Wafs who have been assigned to her flight.

At mealtime the members of a flight march to the dining hall together. The food, served cafeteria style, is attractive and abundant. There are salads, meats, vegetables, desserts, breads, milk, tea, coffee and ice cream. Hamburgers, french fries and soft drinks are available for those who aren't hungry enough for a full meal. Each girl is free to choose what she wants. She will eat at a table for four.

During her first day at Lackland a new Waf meets the training instructor assigned to her flight. The training instructor is an experienced Waf who has taken special courses to help her prepare recruits for their life in the Air Force. The training instructor will remain with the flight for the entire six weeks of basic training. She will quickly get to know the girls' names and something about their backgrounds. It will be her job to show the recruits how things are done in the Air Force and to explain why they should be done that way. She has an assistant, another specially trained Waf. Their goal is to have every member of the flight successfully complete basic training.

One of the highlights of a Waf's first day at Lackland is the assignment of dormitory space. This is where the new Waf will live for six weeks. At Lackland the dormitories are modern, air-conditioned buildings that contain a mailroom, laundry room, television room, supply room, cafeteria, dispensary, classrooms and offices, in addition to sleeping and bathing facilities. Blankets and linens are issued to the recruits. Each girl is also assigned lockers in which to store her personal belongings.

Recruits arrive at Lackland in civilian attire, but they soon receive their Air Force uniforms. The basic WAF uniform is a dark blue suit with a double-breasted jacket and an A-line skirt. It is worn with a light blue blouse that has a dark blue tab at the collar. Other uniform items include black pumps, a black handbag, a dark blue raincoat, a dark blue windbreaker and dark blue slacks.

During her six weeks at Lackland, a recruit receives instruction in a wide range of subjects. She will be introduced to Air Force history, customs and courtesies. She will study military law, first aid and human relations. She will also attend physical training classes and learn the fundamentals of military drill.

Elsewhere at Lackland, male recruits will be studying many of the same subjects. They, however, will learn to use a rifle, and their physical training will be more rigorous.

Women recruits take a special charm and personal hygiene course designed to improve poise, posture and grooming. They learn how to plan a wardrobe, use makeup effectively and select food for a well-balanced diet.

Leisure time is limited during basic training, but the recruit does have some free hours to use as she wishes. Worship services for all denominations are held at the chapel center. There are also evening rap sessions and singalongs at the chapel. A service club offers games, dances and other recreation under the direction of a trained staff. Shopping needs can be taken care of at the base exchange, which resembles a department store.

Recruits take several tests during basic training, usually during the first week. Some of the tests are medical, and others are designed to reveal mental ability and vocational aptitudes. Each recruit is counseled on her special aptitudes and on the Air Force jobs that are currently available. If tests indicate that a recruit has technical ability, she is encouraged

One of the first Wafs to undergo Air Force Security Police training
is directing traffic. Her instructor stands behind her. *(U.S. Air
Force)*

to consider a career in one of the Air Force's many technical job fields.

A WAF recruiter points out: "Women are as guilty of chauvinism as men in thinking of themselves in the traditional career areas—administration, nursing or switchboard operator. We need women in the technical fields—nearly every phase of aircraft systems repair, electronic communication equipment operation and repair and civil engineering. . . . Our major problem now is to convince young women of the desirability of becoming skilled in the technological areas."

Colonel Billie M. Bobbitt, the director of the WAF, notes a change in the job aspirations of Air Force women, however. She observes: "The thing that has impressed me so much in the attitude of the young women line officers, the young enlisted women and the young women medical officers has been the change in what's important to them: their aspirations for jobs, training, assignments, school and advanced education. Now all of a sudden the opportunity is there and they're reaching out for it, whereas there used to be some hangbacks, some hesitancy.

"Not only was it the fear of appearing too masculine, too aggressive, but it has been the fear-of-success syndrome that many women have had in our society in that, if you are a little pushy, a little aggressive, you lose your feminine identity. I think there is less concern for that now. There is now no feeling that there is a conflict between a military career and being feminine. And, of course, I think women are achieving much more as a result of this, and certainly contributing much more; that's what it's all about."

Recruits who did not enlist under the guaranteed job program select their career field during basic training. The Air Force tries to satisfy the career preferences of its women recruits. By law they may not serve as members of combat aircrews. Nor are they assigned to jobs which would be beyond their physical capabilities, or to jobs that would place them in serious jeopardy. Nevertheless, all but seven of the Air Force's 276 enlisted specialties are open to qualified women. The restricted specialties are: combat control team specialist, aircraft loadmaster, security specialist, pararescue/recovery specialist, inflight refueling specialist, flight engineer specialist and defensive fire control specialist. All are combat related.

For some Waf recruits, that eagerly awaited first assignment after basic training will be to a responsible job at one of the Air Force's many installations in the United States. These will be women who already have a skill that the Air Force can use. Any additional training that they need will be obtained while they work. The Armed Forces call this "on-the-job training." In some cases the Waf who receives training will later have an opportunity to obtain advanced training at an Air Force school. However, many enlisted Wafs receive vocational training at an Air Force school before they report to their first duty assignment. Whichever route she follows, the Waf has begun the combination of education and work experience that will allow her to make the most of her abilities. Later, if she should decide to leave the Armed Forces, she will have a head start on a civilian career.

The Waf who becomes an Air Force weather observer will

help determine what weather-influenced Air Force operations can or cannot be attempted. She will observe sky conditions, determine the height and amount of cloud cover, measure visibilities, wind velocities, pressures and temperatures, and operate radar storm detection equipment. In addition to observing and recording weather elements, she will plot weather maps and charts, assemble data for historical weather records and operate weather data machines. Using her observations and records, an Air Force weather forecaster will be able to make her predictions.

To become an Air Force weather observer, a Waf must achieve a score of at least 80 on the Airman Qualifying Examination which is graded on a 0–95 scale. She must also complete the sixteen-week weather observer training course at Chanute Air Force Base, Illinois.

The Air Force is justifiably proud of the way it maintains its planes for safe operation. But it also supplies its aircrews with the equipment they will need in an emergency and makes sure that the fliers know how to use it. A Waf assigned to instruct Air Force crew members in the use of emergency equipment is a protective equipment specialist.

Wafs with this specialty brief fliers on the purpose, operation and care of their oxygen masks, headgear and anti-G suits (a special suit designed to protect a flier from the effects of rapid acceleration or deceleration). The proper use of parachutes, bailout cylinders, life rafts and vests, anti-exposure suits, first-aid kits and emergency food supplies are also included in the course of instruction.

Protective equipment specialists check, fit and adjust emergency equipment, including equipment installed aboard aircraft. They make minor repairs if they are required. They also brief aircrews on the kinds of equipment needed for an upcoming mission and issue the equipment to the crews. If a Waf attains a score of at least 40 on the Airman Qualifying Examination, she can become a protective equipment specialist. Before reporting for duty in her specialty, she will attend a mandatory eight-week training course at Chanute Air Force Base. During her training she will learn how to use emergency equipment and how to instruct aircrews in its use. She will also learn how to inspect and adjust equipment and how to make minor repairs. When she takes up her duties as a protective equipment specialist, she is prepared to play an important part in safeguarding the lives of Air Force fliers.

Air Force electricians install, inspect and repair the many different kinds of low-voltage electrical and electronic equipment used on Air Force bases. A Waf who scores at least 50 on the Airman Qualifying Examination and who is interested in electricity and electronics can apply for training in this specialty.

Most electricians receive their training on the job under the supervision of journeyman electricians. However, the Air Force trains some of its electricians at a nine-week course taught at Sheppard Air Force Base at Wichita Falls, Texas.

Whether she trains on the job or at Sheppard, the novice electrician will learn the fundamentals of electricity. She will learn how to install and maintain interior electrical systems and how to install and care for motors and other equipment. She will learn how to use testing devices, hand tools, solder-

An Air Force Security Police trainee practices firing a .38-caliber revolver from a prone position. *(U.S. Air Force)*

ing irons, tubing and conduit benders, and conduit-threading machines.

At her Air Force post the Waf electrical specialist will use her training to install new equipment and repair equipment that is out of commission. She may have to clean motors and other electrical apparatus, replace faulty parts, make adjustments and work with electronic detection and warning devices.

Wafs who are radio operators help maintain vital communications between Air Force planes and aircraft controllers on the ground. They operate radio receiving and transmitting equipment, tuning receivers to the correct frequencies and changing transmitting frequencies as required. In addition to receiving and transmitting messages, they log, route and relay radio traffic and continuously monitor some radio frequencies.

Air Force radio operators must attain a score of at least 60 on their Airman Qualifying Examination. A ten-week radio operator course taught at Keesler Air Force Base at Biloxi, Mississippi, is recommended, but not required. At that base, students learn the fundamentals of air-to-ground and point-to-point communication by voice. They also receive instruction in inspecting, tuning and operating ground radio receivers and in maintaining radio records and logs.

Flight data recorders, drift meters, pressure gauges and position indicators are some of the instruments handled by the Waf who is an instrument repairman. It is her job to insure that an aircraft's instruments give accurate readings. She installs the instruments, inspects them and makes repairs when they are defective. Her responsibility extends to wiring and electrical connections, which she checks and repairs or replaces if necessary.

A fourteen-week course at Chanute Air Force Base trains instrument repairmen for their specialty. To be eligible for the training, a Waf must score at least 40 on her Airman Qualifying Examination. At Chanute she will learn how aircraft instruments work, how to use test equipment and how to make repairs and adjustments.

Helicopter mechanics must be thoroughly familiar with their craft because they are responsible for the maintenance of everything from the rotor blades to the landing gear.

The Waf who becomes a helicopter mechanic learns her trade at Sheppard Air Force Base where she takes a fourteen-week training course. At Sheppard she is introduced to the fundamentals of helicopter mechanics, with emphasis on the kinds of helicopters used by the Air Force.

On the flight line a helicopter mechanic conducts preflight, postflight and periodic inspections. The inspections include the entire craft—engines, instruments, rotor blades, controls, landing gear, the fuel system and other helicopter systems. If a pilot has reported trouble with the craft, the mechanic checks out the complaint. She removes and replaces defective parts and keeps detailed records of all work performed. Mechanics are also responsible for moving and parking helicopters.

To be eligible for assignment as a helicopter mechanic, a Waf must score at least 50 on the Airman Qualifying Examination.

Today's pilots have to be proficient in the use of aircraft instruments, and Air Force pilots are no exception. To help them, the Air Force uses devices called instrument trainers that reproduce an airplane's instrument panel. The technician who operates an instrument trainer is called an instrument trainer specialist.

A Waf who wishes to become an instrument trainer specialist must score at least 80 on the Airman Qualifying Examination. If she is selected, she will be sent to Chanute Air Force Base for a 29-week training course. She studies basic electronics, the principles of flight and techniques of instruction. Each aircraft has its special trainer, and the student at Chanute learns how to operate and repair several of them.

When her training has been completed, the instrument trainer specialist reports to one of the many Air Force bases where pilots are assigned. She may work with new pilots who are learning to fly or with experienced pilots who are improving their instrument flying capability.

Before a pilot arrives for a training session, the instrument trainer specialist makes sure that her trainer is functioning properly. She does this by "flying" it herself to check the controls and instruments. When the pilot is in the trainer, the instrument trainer specialist produces instrument readings, audible signals and other navigational aids to which her student reacts. Through practice in the trainer the student learns to make the correct response of the skilled pilot. The instrument trainer specialist, therefore, plays an important role in preparing Air Force pilots for their flying duties.

Men and women who maintain law and order on an Air Force base are law enforcement specialists. They admit employees and visitors to the base, protect base personnel and property, apprehend violators of military regulations, investigate minor offenses and traffic accidents that occur on the base, enforce traffic regulations and control base traffic.

The Waf who becomes a law enforcement specialist will spend some of her time driving a patrol vehicle. She will also help compile accident, law violation and other reports and she will assist in the operation of her unit's radio and telephone switchboards.

Law enforcement specialists, who must score at least 40 on the Airman Qualifying Examination, receive their training at Lackland Air Force Base. During five busy weeks they study law enforcement administration, investigative techniques, traffic control, disaster control, riot control and the use of security police weapons.

The foregoing are just a few of the many career opportunities that are open to the enlisted Waf. No matter what field she enters, she will serve side by side with male members of the Air Force. She will receive identical training, compete for promotion on an equal footing and command the same pay as others with her rank and time in grade.

WAF officers also have a wide range of occupations from which to choose, and they, too, can expect to compete for training opportunities, assignments and promotions on an equal basis with their male counterparts.

To prepare for her career as a WAF officer, the young woman who is a college graduate attends the Air Force's School of Military Science, Officer (SMSO) at Lackland Air Force Base. A prospective WAF officer who is still in college can enroll in the Air Force Reserve Officer Training Corps (AFROTC) if there is a unit at her school or at a nearby college. During the 1973–74 school year approximately 2,000 college women were enrolled in 154 AFROTC units. AFROTC has been open to women since 1969, and they are eligible to participate in all phases of the program except flight training.

SMSO applicants must be United States citizens between 20½ and 29½ years old, in good physical condition and able to pass the Air Force Officer Qualifying Test. A baccalaureate degree is required, but college seniors who are about to graduate can apply.

Women who are accepted for SMSO spend three months at Lackland Air Force Base acquiring the military knowledge they will need as newly commissioned Air Force officers. Their stay at Lackland begins with a series of examinations and orientation briefings. Most of their time, however, is devoted to classroom work. The officer candidates learn how the Air Force is organized, what its mission is and what their own responsibilities will be when they become Air Force officers. They study the principles and techniques of leadership, effective oral and written communication and the military justice system.

Career orientation is an important part of SMSO. It acquaints the officer candidate with the career field she will be entering once she is commissioned. A physical training program insures that she remains in top physical condition and drills, ceremonies and inspections help her learn the basic military formations.

During her first few weeks at SMSO, the candidate will receive her WAF officer uniforms. Once she has them, she will wear the appropriate uniform whenever she is on duty. Learning how to wear the uniform and how to take care of it will be part of her SMSO training. The civilian clothing that the candidate brought with her to Lackland can be worn when she is off duty.

The WAF officer uniform resembles that of the enlisted woman. The insignia, however, are different. Until she is commissioned and authorized to wear the gold bars of a second lieutenant, the candidate wears insignia that indicates she is a SMSO student.

With the exception of physical training, women officer candidates attend classes with male candidates, who also receive their initial training at Lackland. Although women are a minority at SMSO, they receive no special treatment and are expected to meet the same standards as male candidates.

Instead of waiting until she graduates from college to begin her WAF officer training, a young woman who attends a school that has an Air Force Reserve Officer Training Corps unit can participate in a two- or four-year training program while she is working for her degree. If she completes the AFROTC requirements, which include two years in the professional officer course and a four- to six-week summer field training course, she will receive her commission as a second lieutenant in the U.S. Air Force when she graduates. She will not be commissioned before she is 21 and all commissioning requirements must be met before her 30th birthday.

AFROTC is coeducational, with men and women receiving the same instruction and training. However, women are not required to participate in small arms marksmanship training, survival indoctrination, or aircraft orientation flights, but they may do so if they wish. Both men and women are eligible to participate in the Air Force's scholarship program for its ROTC students.

Applicants for the AFROTC program must be free of academic probation of any kind. They must pass the Air Force Officer Qualifying Test and meet the physical requirements for commissioning. A favorable interview with the professor of aerospace studies at her school is another requirement that the AFROTC applicant must satisfy.

Jacqueline Pettishall, the first black woman to earn an officer's commission through AFROTC, was enthusiastic about the program. When she graduated from Agricultural and Technical State University at Greensboro, North Carolina, in 1973, she said: "I wish more young ladies would realize the advantages of being in the program. The opportunities are great and after graduation, I won't be looking for a job."

As much as she enjoys the challenge and excitement of her introduction to the Air Force at SMSO or in the AFROTC program, the officer candidate looks forward to the time when her preliminary training is over and she can move on to her first assignment as a commissioned Air Force officer. The Air Force will consider aptitude, experience, education and special training as well as its own needs in determining her assignment. These are the same criteria used in assigning male officers. Women, however, are not assigned to duty as pilots, navigator/observers or missile operations launch officers. Nor are they given assignments that require unusual strength or assignments that would place them in serious physical jeopardy.

Six specialties in the intelligence field are open to qualified WAF officers. They are: intelligence staff officer, intelligence officer, air targets officer, air tactical intelligence officer, signals officer and intelligence photo-radar officer.

Intelligence officers plan and organize activities in their area of specialization and coordinate their work with other Air Force intelligence efforts. They obtain various documents and publications and prepare intelligence summaries. An intelligence officer's duties may involve briefing and debriefing aircraft crews, questioning captured enemy soldiers and civilians and working with cryptographic systems.

The Waf who wishes to become an intelligence officer should have a bachelor's degree in political science, geopolitics, international affairs, civil or architectural engineering, geography, photogrammetry, psychology, foreign service, statistics or in a foreign language. The kind of degree she has will determine her specialty. Whatever her assignment, the Air Force will probably give her additional training to enhance her value as an intelligence officer. Most of the career fields to which the Air Force assigns its officers require some additional training.

Computer technology is one of the newest career fields for Air Force officers. A Waf who has a bachelor's degree in computer sciences, mathematics, business administration, industrial management or engineering management is eligible to become an Air Force computer specialist. She may be assigned as a computer systems design engineer, a computer systems analyst, a computer systems programming officer or a computer systems operations officer. Depending upon her assignment, she may be called upon to design or modify components for a computer system, arrange for the acquisition of a computer system or manage the operation of an Air Force computer facility.

If a WAF officer has a bachelor's degree in science, she is eligible for assignment to a scientific career field. The Air Force uses the services of mathematicians, physicists, chemists, metallurgists and general scientists. These officers plan and conduct research projects that will help the Air Force carry out its mission. Their work often calls for cooperation with the scientific staffs of other government agencies and with contractors doing business with the Air Force.

Another career field open to the WAF officer who has a bachelor's degree in science is that of weather officer. A degree in engineering also makes her eligible for this field. In

Photographed during a training exercise, an enlisted Waf
aeromedical technician sits beside a litter in an Air Force ambu-
lance. The duties of an aeromedical technician include emergency
air evacuation of sick and injured patients and being on call as a
member of a helicopter rescue team trained to help survivors of
aircraft accidents. *(U.S. Air Force)*

both cases she must have 24 college-level semester hours in meteorology.

The Air Force weather officer analyzes weather data, prepares and issues weather forecasts and briefs pilots and others on weather conditions. In some cases she may be in charge of an Air Force weather detachment.

Development engineering is another field that attracts WAF officers who have a degree in science. Depending on her field of specialization, a Waf may be assigned as an aeronautical engineer, an electronics engineer, a mechanical engineer, an astronautical engineer or a special development engineer. Her duties could include conducting research and experiments in her specialty, planning projects, drawing up design and performance standards, and analyzing materiel, techniques and systems used by the Air Force.

WAF officers who have a degree in education or psychology are eligible for the education and training career field. As education and training officers they plan and direct programs for improving the technical qualifications and educational levels of Air Force men and women.

Captain Terrell Berkovsky, who had a degree in education, received an assignment as the commander of a squadron of Wafs. "I thoroughly enjoy military life and like my job," she said. "It's always interesting because dealing with people is enjoyable. There is a constant changeover in girls and though the problems always seem to be the same with each new group, I never get a chance to be bored. I think it's because the majority of the girls are between eighteen and twenty, and they're just finding out what life is all about.

They're refreshing, full of surprises and fascinating to watch."

In intelligence, computer technology, the sciences, education and training and its many other career fields, the Air Force is proud of the opportunities it offers women to use their professional capabilities right from the start. Instead of having to work her way up from the steno pool, as is often the case in a civilian company, the WAF officer puts her college education and her Air Force training to work immediately. And her career progression is based on her performance. In the Air Force her opportunities for advancement are the same as those for men.

# 5

## WOMEN ON
## THE MARCH
## IN THE ARMY

The young woman who joins the United States Army as an enlisted Wac receives her initial training at the WAC Center at Fort McClellan, Alabama, or at Fort Jackson, South Carolina. The WAC Center is a 300-acre complex of modern classroom buildings, living quarters and parks, located in the foothills of the Appalachian Mountains, six miles northeast of Anniston, Alabama. Prior to 1974 all enlisted Wacs reported there for basic training. Fort Jackson at Columbia, South Carolina, was opened for Wac training in 1974 to accommodate an increase in enlistments. At either location the Wac recruit will undergo an eight-week training program that is designed to produce a disciplined and highly motivated young woman who is prepared and qualified to serve as a member of the United States Army.

During her first few days at her basic training center, recruit reports for medical and dental examinations, receives her uniforms and identification cards and takes the aptitude tests that will help determine her assignment when she has completed basic training. She also begins her military training. There is instruction in the fundamentals of drill, how to perform military housekeeping chores, how to mark clothing and how to wear and take care of the WAC uniform.

Wacs wear a gray-green, two-piece, tailored suit and a beige cotton blouse with a black tab. The warm-weather uniform is a short-sleeved, two-piece suit of green cord. Both uniforms are worn with black pumps. The WAC cap is green. Also included in the uniform issue is a green chesterfield-type overcoat and a raincoat.

Each newly arrived recruit is assigned to a training platoon of 34 to 40 women. A recruit lives in a dormitory-style building where her platoon has its own area, called a bay. The bays contain no partitions, but each trainee has her own space with a bed and storage lockers. Trainees eat in large mess halls where food is served cafeteria style. They sit at tables for four.

During her eight weeks of basic training a recruit is introduced to the achievements and traditions of the Army, military customs and courtesies, and the military justice system. She studies first aid, land navigation, Army organization and administration, the principles of leadership, and military field operations. She also receives instruction in such subjects as nutrition and diet, hair care, drug abuse, and problems of group living.

Not all of a basic trainee's time is spent in the classroom.

urs is devoted to learning marching move-
ipating in parades and ceremonies. Another
ned to a physical training program whose
strength, stamina, flexibility and coordina-

...... ..... at both marching and physical training. Major General Charles Hixon, Fort Jackson's commander, remarked: "The women . . . in the first week in training, they're all in step. They're easier to train, oh yes. When we say jump, the question they ask is: 'Is that high enough?' "

During the fifth week of basic training, two days are spent in the field. The exercise includes night and day marches and, when the weather permits, the trainees sleep in tents which they have learned to pitch. On one day of each week the trainees perform various housekeeping chores. They work in a mess hall, cut grass and pick up litter. Each trainee also takes her turn at helping to clean her barracks and acting as charge-of-quarters.

After the first week of basic training, recruits are eligible for a pass which permits them to leave the training area for a few hours. After the second week, they are allowed to use a service club where recreation facilities include a snack bar, game, music and TV rooms, kitchens and an outdoor patio. During the summer a swimming pool is available for trainee use. After the fourth week of training, recruits may earn a pass which permits them to leave the military installation. They may not remain away overnight, however.

Basic trainees undergo frequent inspections of their living areas, clothing and personal appearance. They earn points for performance in inspections as well as for their classroom work. The minimum attainment for successful completion of basic training is 700 of a possible 1,000 points. Trainees who fail to achieve the necessary 700 points may be allowed to drop back into another training platoon for a second chance to succeed. However, most trainees will earn the necessary 700 points. For them, graduation will come on the Friday of the eighth week of training. There will be a graduation parade followed by a ceremony in the WAC chapel to which the friends and relatives of the graduating class are invited.

Once basic training has been completed, the new Wac who already has a skill that the Army can use is ready to report to her first post. Any additional training that she needs will be obtained while she works and she will be eligible for advanced training later. For most Wacs, however, basic training is followed by several weeks of training at one of the Army's technical schools. Women attend these schools on an equal basis with men assigned to the same occupational specialty.

Only 48 of the Army's 482 enlisted occupational specialties are closed to women. All of the 48 are combat related. "This is not to say that [women] will not serve where they are in danger as they did in Korea and South Vietnam," a director of the WAC has pointed out.

The 434 specialties that are open to enlisted members of the WAC provide them with a choice of jobs in such varied fields as administration, air operations support, drafting, food service, finance, supply, communications, intelligence, data processing and music.

A Wac's assignment to an occupational specialty is determined by the aptitude tests that she has taken, interviews

From her control tower overlooking the Pentagon's landing pad, an enlisted Wac aircraft controller communicates with the pilot of a helicopter. *(U.S. Army)*

with counselors about her abilities and job preferences and the needs of the Army. In some cases she will have been guaranteed the job of her choice when she enlisted.

While Army regulations prohibit a Wac from being assigned to a job that would require her to fly in combat aircraft, she is eligible for a number of responsible jobs in Army aviation. Enlisted Wacs work as air traffic control tower operators, as ground control approach specialists, air traffic control en route specialists, air traffic control chiefs and flight simulator specialists. Wac meteorological observers gather the weather data that the Army needs to conduct its air operations.

Enlisted Wacs who can play brass, woodwind or percussion instruments are eligible for assignment to one of the Army's bands. Enlisted bandleader is another job open to musically talented WAC musicians.

A Wac who has language skills may qualify for an interesting Army career as a translator-interpreter or an expert linguist. Additional training is available to her at one of the Defense Language Institute's schools.

As the operator of one of the world's best medical support systems, the Army has a number of worthwhile career opportunities for qualified women. In Army hospitals, clinics, laboratories and pharmacies enlisted Wacs assist professional personnel in a wide range of medical specialities, including dental care, medical social work, occupational therapy, physical therapy, radiology, orthopedics and pharmacy. They work as medical specialists, clinical specialists and operating room specialists.

A Wac who is interested in photography might become

one of the Army's still photographers or one of its photographic laboratory specialists. Or she might be assigned as a TV production specialist or as an audio specialist.

More than 200 enlisted Wacs are recruiters who assist in the Army's effort to interest qualified young people in military careers. Other Wacs work with recruits as career counselors. Wacs also serve as drill sergeants at the two WAC basic training centers.

Administration is important at all levels of the Army and it is a field that offers many career opportunities for the enlisted Wac who has clerical skills or aptitude. She can become a stenographer, a legal clerk, a court reporter, a personnel specialist, an information specialist or a broadcast specialist.

Specialist 5 Gracie Gibbs, the first Wac to become a member of the Army's elite Special Forces, received her assignment because of her administrative specialty. Along with the assignment to the 5th Special Forces Group Headquarters at Fort Bragg, North Carolina, came the right to wear the Special Forces crest on the epaulet of her uniform and the Special Forces arrowhead-shaped patch. "It makes me stand a little taller when I'm in a group of other Wacs," she said.

These are just some of the jobs that are part of Army administration. In them, and in the other Army specialties open to her, the enlisted Wac will compete on an equal basis with men for training opportunities and advancement.

Newly commissioned WAC officers spend eleven weeks at the WAC Center at Fort McClellan learning the fundamentals of Army life. Their formal training begins after several days of processing, during which they are interviewed by

WAC Center administrators and faculty advisers. The student officers attend their first briefings and they report to the Center's dispensary for physical and dental examinations. They also purchase their uniforms and make arrangements for any alterations that might be needed.

Each new officer receives an allowance for the purchase of uniforms at the WAC clothing sales store. The actual cost of the required uniforms exceeds the allowance, however, and she will have to pay the difference herself.

Items in the WAC officer's military wardrobe include a gray-green wool suit for winter, which is worn with a cream-beige blouse, a matching gray-green hat with a rounded crown, a two-piece green and white cord summer uniform, a gray-green chesterfield-style overcoat with a removable lining and a raincoat, also with a removable lining. For official functions and social occasions that require a uniform, the WAC officer wears a "dress blues" suit of soft blue wool or a white suit of Dacron or gabardine. For formal evening occasions, she wears a jacket and skirt of midnight blue or frost-white broadcloth with a matching cummerbund of silk faille and a ruffled white blouse. The skirt for formal evening wear may be either long or short.

While she attends the orientation course at the WAC Center, the student officer lives in comfortable bachelor officer quarters where she shares a room with another student. Each room has two beds, a bookcase, desk, lounge chair and storage space for military and civilian clothing. A large living room, kitchen and laundry facilities are available for student use.

At the WAC Center the school day usually begins at 7:30

in the morning and ends at 4:30 in the afternoon. In classes that normally run 50 minutes in length, the student officers are introduced to the history and traditions of the Army. Lecturers outline the Army's role in national defense and explain how the Army is organized to carry out its mission. The students learn the importance to the Army's mission of communications, supply, personnel management, administration, intelligence and other fields to which they might be assigned when they finish their training. They also become familiar with Army terminology, military courtesies and customs and the military justice system.

Leadership training is an important part of a WAC officer's military education. During the orientation course at the WAC Center, students participate in discussions in which they examine the responsibilities of the Army officer, various methods of handling personnel problems and other aspects of leadership.

Like all military students, the WAC officer candidate is required to take part in a physical training program. She also learns drill and command techniques. Although she will probably never be directly involved in combat, she might be caught in a combat situation. Therefore, the Army teaches her how to react to chemical and nuclear attacks, how to treat victims of such attacks, how to use camouflage and other protective measures.

As is the case with the other military services, the Army obtains some of its officers through its Reserve Officer Training Corps program for college and university students who earn an Army commission by taking ROTC courses and training while they are studying for a baccalaureate degree.

(The Army's Military Academy, like the Air Force Academy, the Naval Academy and the Coast Guard Academy, which also supply officers for the Armed Forces, has not yet been opened to women.)

The Army opened its Reserve Officer Training Corps to women, in 1972, in an experiment that involved ten schools distributed across the country. The move proved so successful that it was extended the next year to all colleges and universities having an Army ROTC unit.

Women cadets participate in the same Army ROTC program as do male cadets: a basic course during their freshman and sophomore years, followed by an advanced course during the junior and senior years. Between the junior and senior years cadets attend an advanced summer camp. A two-year program with a basic summer camp replacing the first two years of on-campus training is also available.

ROTC cadets in the advanced course receive $100 for each month they are in school for up to ten months of the year and an additional $400 for attending the advanced summer camp.

Women enrolling in the ROTC program are eligible to compete for scholarships that pay for tuition, textbooks, and laboratory fees and provide a $100 monthly allowance for ten months of the year, the same benefits as those received by male scholarship holders. Two-, three- and four-year scholarships are available.

In return for their monthly allowance, nonscholarship ROTC students must serve at least two years on active duty after they graduate. The service obligation of scholarship students varies with the amount of aid received, ranging up to a four-year service obligation for a full four-year scholarship.

As members of an Army ROTC unit, women drill, study military tactics, stand inspection, fire on target ranges with male cadets and compete with men for positions as cadet company officers. ROTC activities require from three to five hours of a student's time each week.

Women who successfully fulfill the requirements of the ROTC program receive their Army commission when they graduate and they report for active duty as second lieutenants.

The Army has two additional programs for college women who are considering a military career. One is the College Junior Course, which gives women who have completed their junior year a preview of the opportunities that are available to them as WAC officers. College women who qualify for this program spend four summer weeks at the WAC Center as cadet corporals in the WAC Enlisted Reserve. With cadets from all over the country, they participate in a course of instruction that includes classroom work, drill, and physical training. There is also a field trip to the U.S. Army Infantry Center at Fort Benning, Georgia.

Each cadet in the College Junior Course is provided with uniforms, meals and medical care. The Army also pays for the cadet's transportation to the WAC Center and back home again. In addition, a cadet receives the pay of an Army corporal while she is at the WAC Center.

During their four weeks at the Center, cadets meet WAC officers, observe them at work and take part in Center social activities. From their contacts with WAC officers and their

In an Army recording studio in Washington, D.C., a Wac information-tion specialist records material for use by military radio stations. *(U.S. Army)*

formal course of instruction, they learn what to expect from a career in the Army. At the same time, the Army has a chance to evaluate the cadets as potential WAC officers.

Cadets who participate in the College Junior Course are under no obligation to continue in the Enlisted Reserve. But a girl who is convinced that she would like to become an officer in the Women's Army Corps can apply for admission to the Army's Student Officer Program. Each year a limited number of applicants are selected for this program from among those who received the highest rating in the College Junior Course.

Participants in the Student Officer Program are members of the U.S. Army Reserve during their senior year in college. They receive the pay and allowances of a corporal, and other benefits, such as medical and dental care, but they perform no military duties. They do assume the obligation to serve at least two years of active duty as a WAC officer.

Six months before graduation, Officer Program students apply for a second lieutenant's commission which is awarded when they graduate. The new lieutenants then report to the WAC Center for officer orientation.

After their eleven weeks of officer orientation at the WAC Center, women officers attend the basic officer course of one of the other branches of the Army. Including the Women's Army Corps, there are 24 such branches. Only three of them, Armor, Infantry and Field Artillery, are closed to women for this phase of their training. Among the branches whose basic officer course women may attend are the Corps of Engineers, the Finance Corps, the Quartermaster Corps, the Chemical Corps, the Transportation Corps, the Intelligence and

Security Branch, and the Judge Advocate General's Corps. When she graduates from her basic officer course, the WAC officer is ready for her first duty assignment. Tests and interviews have established her abilities and preferences and they are taken into consideration, along with the needs of the Army, in determining her assignment. In some cases she will need specialized training before she takes up her new duties, or she will become eligible for advanced training later. She will receive this additional training at the same schools that male officers attend.

The Wac who is assigned as an intelligence officer becomes a part of the Army's worldwide intelligence network that gathers and analyzes data about foreign countries for military planning and operations purposes. Some intelligence officers become psychological warfare experts who prepare information for distribution in war zones by means of radio, the press and other media.

WAC officers who are recruiters work with the young men and women who are investigating the possibilities of an Army career. The WAC officer who is assigned to this field interviews, evaluates and processes prospective members of the Army. Her duties will also require her to visit schools, make speeches and arrange exhibits.

Officers assigned to WAC company positions at the WAC Center play a very important role in preparing women for their careers in the Army. Some of these officers are involved with the reception and processing of newly arrived recruits. Others are assigned as teachers. WAC units at posts throughout the Army are in charge of WAC company officers who must see that the members of the unit are well housed, well fed, paid and given career and personal counseling.

Administration is a field that offers an unusual number of opportunities for the talented WAC officer. In the Army, administration has many facets—records management, data processing, editing and printing a wide variety of publications and controlling correspondence are some of them. The WAC officer assigned to administration has much the same job as an office manager in private business.

Personnel is another field that offers many career opportunities for the WAC officer. The Wac who is a personnel officer deals with the Army's men and women. She may act as a counselor; she may be responsible for the aptitude testing that helps determine assignments; she may plan recruiting and training programs based on the Army's present and future needs; or she may help evaluate Army personnel for promotion.

For the creative Wac officer, information is a rewarding career field. As the information officer at an Army post, she will write news releases for the public press, help edit an Army newspaper, arrange for tours of the post and assist in the reception of important visitors. She will also be the post commander's public relations adviser.

Although all Army women, other than officers in the health fields, are required to be members of the Women's Army Corps, they are very much a part of the Army. Once they have completed basic training or WAC officer orientation they are, with the exception of combat-related schools and jobs, assigned to the same schools and occupational fields as men. On the job, Wacs do the same work, have the same responsibilities and receive the same pay and benefits as male members of the Army.

Moreover, women are now filling some of the Army's formerly all-male command positions. A WAC colonel has successfully commanded the 2,500 members, mostly male, of the Headquarters Support Command at Fort Jackson, South Carolina. In 1972, the first Wac to attend the Army's field artillery officer career course reported for class at Fort Sill, Oklahoma. She was preparing for an assignment as the commander of a field artillery unit.

When asked what he thought about a woman taking the course, which had been restricted to males, one of her classmates said: "Why shouldn't she go through the course and get the MOS [military occupation specialty]? Sex, the same as race, has to be eliminated as a barrier to job opportunities. I think most of the guys feel the same way. If (she) can, why not let her do it? I think it's great!"

Another classmate said: "She can do any job a man can in field artillery. I don't think it's necessary for the officer to be a man just so he can cuss the troops out to get them moving. But I'm not saying that every woman can command —neither can every man. It depends on individuals and their particular talents. What I'm saying is that a woman can perform any job she's trained for as well as a man can."

In discussing the leadership potential of military women, WAC Lieutenant Colonel Nancy Hopfenspirger, who commanded the Army's 830-man Würzburg Support Activity, in Germany, also pointed out that the important question for the Army is whether a leader possesses the qualities neces-

One of the Army's military policewomen talks with her radio dispatcher. Military police is one of the career fields opened to women when the Army made all but combat-related and extremely hazardous or arduous jobs available to them. *(U.S. Army)*

sary to accomplish a unit's mission, not whether the leader is a man or a woman.

Enlisted women are also moving into formerly all-male preserves. A Wac has been first sergeant of the male student company at the Army's Aberdeen Proving Ground, in Maryland. Wacs have taken parachute training at the Army's jump school at Fort Benning, Georgia. They have become military police, truck drivers and heavy equipment operators.

Speaking for her sister Wacs, Sergeant First Class Addie Barnes declared: "We want to prove that we can do the jobs that men have monopolized for so many years."

"As I see the Army of the 70s," said Brigadier General Mildred C. Bailey, Director of the WAC, "we really will achieve true integration of our men and women as coworkers and contributors to the Army's mission, with mutual respect, understanding and acceptance."

# 6

## WOMEN ON
## THE MARCH
## IN THE NAVY

The United States Navy maintains two schools for women who are beginning a naval career. One of the schools, located at Orlando, Florida, gives enlisted women their basic training. The other, at Newport, Rhode Island, is for officer candidates.

At Orlando, the Navy's women recruits spend a busy nine weeks studying Navy organization, history, customs and traditions. They are introduced to the Navy's "language." Floors are "decks" in the Navy, walls are "bulkheads," kitchens are "galleys," and the recruits live in "quarters." Military time is different, too. Like recruits in the other services, a Wave learns to use the military 24-hour-clock system of telling time. She will say 1000 (ten hundred) when it's 10 A.M., 1700 (seventeen hundred) when it's 5 P.M. and 2130 (twenty-one thirty) when it's 9:30 P.M. And she will learn that a ship or station bell strikes once for each half-hour of a four-hour period, the day being divided into six periods, or watches, of four hours each.

A Wave recruit learns to identify the different kinds of ships that the Navy uses to accomplish its mission. She adds CVA (for attack aircraft carrier), CA (for heavy cruiser) and SSN (for submarine, nuclear) to her growing vocabulary of Navy terms. She also learns to identify the Navy's weapons and the planes flown by Navy airmen.

Because the Navy expects its women to keep fit, physical training is emphasized at the Naval Training Center along with swimming and water safety. Recruits also receive instruction in poise and grooming and in the correct wearing of their new uniforms.

Shortly after she arrives at Orlando, a recruit receives her basic uniforms. The dress blue uniform is a navy blue wool suit with gold buttons. It is worn with a white blouse and black tie. For summer, there is a white uniform designed in the same style as the dress blue one, and a blue, short-sleeved, two-piece suit of Dacron. The uniform issue also includes hats, purses, gloves, an overcoat, a raincoat and other items. After she acquires her uniforms, a recruit appears in the correct uniform whenever she is on duty. She may continue to wear civilian clothing during her off-duty hours, however.

Although the training program at the Orlando Naval Center keeps recruits busy, from early morning until their evening meal, with classroom work, dormitory duties and student company responsibilities, they do have off-duty time during which they can use the Center's recreational facilities.

While she is at the Naval Training Center, each recruit

takes a series of classification tests to determine her vocational aptitudes. She will also be interviewed by a counselor who will tell her about the special training programs for which she might be eligible when she has finished basic training. Her assignment to a rating ("rating" is the Navy's term for an occupational field) will be determined by her interests and aptitudes, and the needs of the Navy.

Under the equal rights and opportunities policy adopted by the Navy in 1972, enlisted women are eligible for all Navy ratings, although in some cases their numbers are limited. Moreover, Navy commanders have been directed to insure that women are allowed to perform the duties for which they have been trained. Admiral Elmo Zumwalt, Jr., chief of Naval Operations, in an equal rights and opportunities message to the Navy's commanders, said: "I believe that we can do far more than we have in the past in according women equal opportunity to contribute their extensive talents and to achieve full professional status."

With all ratings open to them, enlisted women fill a variety of administrative, scientific, technical and medical jobs in the Navy's shore establishment. And in 1972, 62 enlisted Waves went to sea as crew members of the hospital ship *Sanctuary,* in a pilot program designed to prepare the way for the assignment of women to more Navy ships. By law, seagoing assignments for Navy women have been limited to hospital and transport vessels, but a change in that law appears likely.

Several of the women assigned to the *Sanctuary* attended the Navy's firefighting school at Treasure Island, California, before reporting for duty aboard ship. During their training they had to take fire-fighting equipment into a mockup ship's

When this photo was taken, one of the Waves assigned as a crew-member aboard the *Sanctuary* was training at a Navy fire-fighting school. With two male students she is ready to advance on a simulated shipboard fire. *(U.S. Navy)*

compartment that was engulfed in flames. Later, one of the Waves, Hospital Corpsman Shirley A. Geiling, said: "We felt we couldn't fail. There were too many people watching us. Besides, I felt we could hack it along with the men."

Their instructor was pleased with his *Sanctuary* students who were the first women to attend the fire-fighting school. He remarked: "They were eager and there was very little backsliding."

On the *Sanctuary* 25 of the Waves were assigned as deck hands, twenty-one were medical assistants or dental technicians, three were clerks, one was a radio operator and twelve worked in ship service and supply.

As is the case with the other services, the Navy assigns only men to combat-related jobs. However, this restriction does not prevent women from holding a variety of jobs in naval aviation.

The enlisted Wave who wants to work with airplanes can become an aviation maintenance administrationman. Her duties could include scheduling aircraft inspections, issuing aircraft work orders and inspection forms, maintaining records of aircraft failures, analyzing failure trends, operating a technical library and performing the clerical work that helps to keep the Navy's planes flying.

Aviation maintenance administrationmen are trained at one of the Navy's technical schools or through on-the-job training combined with individual study. The Wave who enters this field could be assigned to a naval air base, to one of the Navy's large aircraft overhaul and repair installations or to staff duty at a major Atlantic or Pacific naval command.

Another of the several aviation-related jobs open to enlisted Waves is that of aviation storekeeper. The Navy's aviation storekeepers order, store, check and distribute aeronautical equipment. Using computers and other office machines, they keep records that indicate what equipment is on hand, what has been ordered and what has been issued to users.

Some aviation storekeepers are trained at a Navy technical school while others train on the job. A woman aviation storekeeper can expect to be assigned to one of the Navy's air stations.

The recruit who is selected for a tradevman (training devices man) rating will help instruct Navy personnel at schools, training centers and air stations. First, however, she will attend the Navy's Avionics Fundamentals School from which selected graduates go on to a tradevman school. If she doesn't go to Tradevman School, a Wave can improve her qualifications for this rating through on-the-job training and individual study.

In order to be selected for tradevman training, a recruit must have above-average general learning ability, including the ability to use numbers in practical problems, and a clear speaking voice. Any courses she may have taken in mathematics, physics, electricity, electronics and shop work will be helpful, but the Navy will teach her what she needs to know.

She will learn enough about physics, electricity and electronics to work with the electronic and electromechanical components of flight simulators and other training equipment. She will be expected to operate, repair and maintain the equipment and use it to instruct individuals or classes. She may also be called upon to train others to use the equipment.

If a Wave is interested in electronics and has an aptitude for detailed mechanical work, she might become a Navy electronics technician. While prior experience in electronics is helpful, it is not required for this rating. What a Wave must have is a good knowledge of arithmetic, normal color perception and an above-average ability to think and learn. If she is selected for training in electronics, the Navy will send her to a service school when she finishes recruit training. She will study basic electricity and electronics, learn how batteries, motors and generators operate and how to use tools and test equipment. When she completes her special training, she will be assigned to one of the Navy's shore establishments. However, if the *Sanctuary* experiment and a change in the law result in more women being assigned to sea duty, some Waves who are electronic technicians could serve on the Navy's ships. The same is true of Waves holding other ratings.

Because radio communication is so important to its operations, the Navy has many openings for radiomen. To be eligible for this rating, a Wave must possess good hearing, manual dexterity and the ability to learn quickly. High school courses in mathematics, physics and typing are helpful, as is amateur radio experience.

Navy radiomen learn their trade through a combination of on-the-job training, individual study and Navy schooling. They become experts in operating, maintaining and testing the equipment used in radiotelephone and radioteletype communications. Those who cannot already do so, must learn to type and all radiomen must be able to use the International Morse Code.

The Wave who becomes a radioman will be assigned to one of the Navy's shore stations. Among her duties will be transmitting, receiving, routing and logging radio messages. She will tune radio transmitters and receivers and she may have to repair defective equipment.

Every military commander needs capable office workers to help him run his installation. In the Navy, these men and women are called yeomen. The Wave who wants to become a yeoman must be able to learn quickly; she should have an aptitude for handling details and the ability to work harmoniously with others.

Yeoman are trained through a combination of on-the-job instruction and school courses to prepare correspondence, assemble reports, maintain files and perform other administrative and secretarial duties. They also learn how to operate office machines. Advanced training is available in several subjects, including stenography, personnel administration and legal procedures.

The Navy's yeomen work at United States naval installations throughout the world.

Dental technology is one of the health-related career fields open to the enlisted Wave. After she has finished recruit training, the Wave who is to become a dental technician attends Dental Technician School where she studies such subjects as dental anatomy, dental diseases and oral hygiene. She will learn how to prepare patients for dental work, how to assist a dentist and how to care for dental equipment.

When a dental technician finishes her training, she will be assigned to a hospital or dispensary at one of the Navy's shore stations.

After 47 years as all-male organizations,the U.S. Navy's bands have opened their ranks to women. The first Wave to become a Navy musician, Petty Officer Evangeline Bailey, had been serving as a hospital corpsman. Upon joining a band as a vocalist, she received a musician's rating.

"I'm excited about joining the band and getting to sing with them," she said of her new assignment. "I feel that everything I do could have an effect on women coming into the band in the future. Everyone is being so nice, and I really am enjoying working with them."

Only applicants who already are proficient as vocalists or instrumentalists are accepted for training as Navy musicians. They attend the Navy School of Music at Norfolk, Virginia, which offers instruction in every aspect of music. Upon completing the course at Norfolk, students are assigned to one of the Navy's musical organizations.

The Navy's Second Class Diving School is another formerly all-male institution that is now open to women. Students at the school study the physics of water and gases, the physical problems associated with diving and how to cope with dangerous forms of marine life and other diving hazards. They become experts in the use of self-contained breathing apparatus.

When they finish their work at the school, which is located in San Diego, California, students are able to dive to a depth of 200 feet wearing a suit and helmet that weighs 84 pounds. Their shoes weigh another 35 pounds, their air hose weighs

20 pounds and they carry an additional 55 pounds of weights. To prepare for what she knew would be strenuous training, Personnelman Seaman Nancy Garner, the first woman to enroll in the diving school, ran three miles and swam from a half to three-quarters of a mile every day. She also lifted weights. Nancy was already a qualified scuba diver. "I've always been athletic," she said. "I looked to diving as a challenge and it certainly was one."

"The school was physically exhausting to say the least," reported Seaman Garner. "The only real problem was trying to keep up with the guys on pushups—there was no slack at all. There was a little sarcasm now and then," she added, "but the guys were real gentlemen. The class spirit helped everyone. Everyone was equal and when you've got a whole class pulling together, now that's all right."

Upon completing her work at the diving school, Seaman Garner expected to train in a technical speciality to prepare for an assignment that would include underwater salvage work.

When asked if she would recommend diving to other women, she said: "Well, the first thing they have to realize is that it's serious business. I think it would be great if another woman wanted to go to the school, but I think she should be mentally as well as physically prepared for it. It takes your entire mind and body, but it's worth it."

In addition to the many career opportunities offered by its regular enlistment programs, the Navy has special programs designed for men and women who have graduated from a vocational or technical school or from a junior college. The Wave who has graduated from a vocational or technical school with the required number of hours of training in a field for which the Navy has a vocational rating can begin her naval career at an advanced pay rate. Recruits who have graduated from a junior college, or completed two years of study beyond high school, can also enter the Navy at an advanced rate. Furthermore, they are eligible for training in electronics, medical and dental science, meteorology, aircraft traffic control, photography and many other highly desirable technical fields.

The Navy's women officers have also discovered that the service's equal opportunity policies have increased the number of desirable jobs open to them. Restrictions on the assignment of women to command positions at shore installations have been lifted. Moreover, two women officers were among the Waves assigned to the *Sanctuary*'s crew. Pilot training, formerly available only to men, has been opened to women on a trial basis. And the Navy considers females as well as males when selecting officers to attend the prestigious National War College and Industrial College of the Armed Forces.

Women college graduates who are candiates for commissions in the Navy attend a nineteen-week training course at the Officer Candidate School, one of several schools at the Naval Officer Training Center at Newport, Rhode Island. The Officer Candidate School is coeducational. Men and women receive their naval indoctrination together, attend the same academic classes, share a sports program, compete for student leadership positions and drill together. However, women are not required to carry rifles when they drill.

Most of an officer candidate's time at Newport is devoted

Two of the first women to be chosen for Navy flight training pose before a T-34 Mentor trainer aircraft. They are holding their flight helmets. *(U.S. Navy)*

to academic studies. The candidate is introduced to naval history and to the organization and function of the U.S. Navy. She learns the principles of personnel management as practiced by the Navy, how the Navy handles its ships, equipment and supplies, how to use the various types of Navy correspondence and how military justice is administered. She will need all of this information as a junior naval officer.

Officer Candidate School also provides its students with the general information about naval tactics that they will need, no matter where they are assigned. The students study the worldwide naval communications network and the security classification system that applies to some Navy communications. They are introduced to the principles of shiphandling and the rules governing ship movement. They also become familiar with the Navy's major weapons systems.

All women enrolled in the Officer Candidate School spend at least one day on a ship at sea. They learn shipboard procedures and observe how the members of the ship's company carry out their duties. They also observe the operation of technical equipment which they have studied in the classroom.

The physical training program for women officer candidates is a less strenuous version of the program for men. It includes body conditioning, first-aid instruction, swimming and water safety instruction and competitive athletics.

While she is at Newport, an officer candidate lives in quarters set aside for students. She shares a room with another woman officer candidate and eats in a nearby dining hall.

An officer candidate's day begins with reveille at 6 A.M.

and ends with lights out at 10:30 P.M. The schedule of student activities includes a daily inspection and six hours of classroom instruction. After a candidate receives her uniforms, she wears the appropriate uniform for school activities. Each student receives an allowance for the purchase of the uniforms that she will need at Officer Candidate School and an additional allowance upon graduation. The uniforms of a woman officer are similar to those issued to enlisted women. The insignia, however, are different.

Students who successfully complete Officer Candidate School are commissioned ensigns in the U.S. Navy when they graduate.

The Navy's Reserve Officer Training Corps programs offer another way for a young woman to prepare for a career in that service. Women have been eligible for NROTC since 1972, when seventeen freshmen women at four universities became NROTC scholarship students. The following year, all NROTC units and the NROTC nonsubsidized college program were opened to women.

Students are chosen for the NROTC scholarship program by a national committee using a quota system that apportions selectees among the states. Applicants must meet physical and other requirements, and be accepted by the school that they wish to attend.

Because they will be assigned to technical career fields in the Navy, women who are NROTC scholarship students select technical or scientific majors, with electrical engineering, electronic engineering, mechanical engineering, data processing, operations research and marine engineering being especially recommended.

During their four years in college, NROTC scholarship students take a number of naval science courses, designed to familiarize them with their chosen service, and they participate in NROTC drills. Three summer training periods are also required. Women normally report to a Navy shore installation for their summer training.

While they are in school, NROTC scholarship students hold the rank of midshipmen in the U.S. Naval Reserve. The Navy pays them $100 a month, pays the cost of tuition and textbooks and furnishes the students' uniforms. In return, the students agree to serve on active duty for at least four years after graduation.

Women enter the Navy's nonsubsidized college program during their freshman or sophomore year in college. They are selected for the program on the basis of personal interviews, recommendations, scholastic records and aptitude tests. Those with technical or scientific majors receive first consideration.

Like the scholarship students, women in the NROTC college program take naval science courses and participate in regular drills. They attend one six-week summer training session.

At the beginning of her junior year, a woman in the college program is sworn in as a midshipman in the Naval Reserve. She then begins to draw a monthly allowance of $100. When she graduates, she becomes an ensign in the Naval Reserve. Her active duty obligation is three years, after which she is released to inactive status in the Navy's Ready Reserve.

Whether she receives her commission through attendance at the Officer Candidate School or participation in one of the

NROTC programs, the woman Navy officer can look forward to duty assignments that will allow her to grow professionally. Moreover, a wide range of challenging jobs will be open to her. Although women are forbidden by law to serve on the Navy's combat vessels, women officers can be assigned to most positions at naval bases, shipyards, test centers, electronics laboratories, supply depots, schools and communications stations.

Women who hold a degree from a recognized law school and have been admitted to the bar are eligible for service with the Navy's Judge Advocate General's Corps. As Navy lawyers, they will handle cases that range from the kind encountered in civilian practice to cases dealing with matters of maritime and international law. A Navy lawyer can be assigned to represent the United States in a case involving an infraction of military law, or she can be assigned to represent an accused member of the Navy.

Navy lawyers have the opportunity to further their legal education at government expense at civilian law schools, the Naval War College and the Armed Forces Staff College.

The woman officer who is assigned to the Navy Supply Corps can become a specialist in financial management, procurement, merchandising, food service, transportation management, inventory management, petroleum management or in operations research and analysis, which includes computer systems management. She will begin her career as a Supply Corps officer at the Navy Supply Corps School in Athens, Georgia, where she will learn how to function as a supply officer at the junior officer level. As her career progresses, she will be encouraged to take advantage of additional training opportunities to improve her chances for promotion.

Women have only recently been admitted to the Navy Civil Engineer Corps. Civil engineers design, construct and maintain the Navy's shore installations. They also buy, manage and sell real estate for the Navy. The woman officer assigned to the Civil Engineer Corps might do any one of these things, or her job might be in some other field, such as public works or military housing. Like her male counterparts, she will have an opportunity for advanced training as she progresses in her civil engineering career.

The Naval School Command, which is responsible for training thousands of Navy men and women, has been commanded by a WAVE captain. Several women officers have taught at the Naval Academy and other Navy schools. Training posts such as these are part of the Navy's personnel field which offers many opportunities for women officers.

Waves hold responsible positions as personnel classification officers, civilian personnel officers, personnel research officers, personnel performance officers, personal affairs officers and procurement and recruiting officers. In these and other jobs in the personnel field, the woman officer can expect to progress to positions of increasing responsibility as she acquires experience and advanced training.

The woman officer who is assigned to the Navy's administrative field might be an administrative assistant, a management analysis officer, a postal officer, a records management officer or a data processing systems analyst. In administration, as in other Navy career fields, a Wave can expect to advance at the same rate as men with the same amount of experience and training.

In 1973, the Navy opened its flight training program to six WAVE officers who became the first women to receive instruction as military aviators. Like the women assigned to the *Sanctuary*'s crew, the six aviation cadets were part of an experiment. When they finished fourteen months of training, they were to report for duty as pilots of helicoptors or multi-engine planes assigned to noncombat search and rescue, and transport missions. After six months, the Navy planned to evaluate the program to determine if more women should become pilots.

The Navy's program for providing equal opportunities for its women has involved changes in organization as well as changes in assignments. There is no longer a WAVE "director," whose official title was assistant chief of naval personnel for women. Women are now included along with men in the Navy's regular command structure.

A proposal to drop the name Waves for Navy women was less successful. Waves, derived from Women Accepted for Volunteer Emergency Service, no longer has any meaning when applied to women who are an important and permanent part of the Navy, but the acronym continues to be used by almost everyone. After its suggestion that the name be dropped was ignored, the Navy gave up. Although they no longer serve on an emergency basis, Navy women are still known as Waves.

# 7

## WOMEN ON
## THE MARCH
## IN THE
## MARINE CORPS

 The woman who joins the U.S. Marine Corps becomes a member of a service that has a high ratio of combat forces to general support forces. This limits the number of career opportunities available to women marines, who are excluded from duty with combat forces. Nevertheless, the Marine Corps is committed to making the maximum use of women's services that its combat-ready mission will permit. In 1973 General Robert E. Cushman, Jr., commandant of the Marine Corps, announced the Corps' goal for its women members. "Our goal," the general said, "is to provide equal opportunity for all women marines and to fully use their abilities in support of Marine Corps objectives."

During eight weeks of strenuous training at its Parris Island, South Carolina, "boot camp," the Marine Corps introduces its women recruits to military life. The Marine Corps also trains some of its male recruits at the large Parris Island base, but men and women recruits attend separate classes.

Shortly after she arrives at Parris Island, a recruit will be assigned to a training platoon. There will be anywhere from 40 to 55 girls in her platoon. An equal number of new arrivals makes up a second platoon. Each platoon has its own living area, which the new marine learns to call a squadbay. In her squadbay, the recruit is assigned a bunk (the Marine term for bed) and storage space. She will eat her meals in the Woman Recruit Training Battalion mess hall.

Within two days after the recruits report to Parris Island, the Marine Corps issues them uniforms. During the remainder of their stay at boot camp, the recruits are expected to appear in the proper uniform. Any civilian clothing that they brought with them will be stored for the duration of recruit training.

The summer uniform of the woman marine is a two-piece green suit of cotton polyester. The winter uniform is a two-piece suit of green wool. Shirts, ties, handbags, caps, gloves, scarf, shoes and raincoat are included in the uniform issue.

During her first few days at Parris Island, a recruit meets many new people. Two of the most important of these new acquaintances are the drill instructors (DI's) assigned to her platoon. They are women marine noncommissioned officers, especially selected for the important job of training recruits. The DI's supervise all aspects of recruit training and evaluate the progress of each member of the platoon.

Recruits lead a busy life at Parris Island. The day begins

with reveille at 5 A.M. By 7:30, a recruit has eaten breakfast and tidied her area of the squadbay. Most of the remainder of the day is taken up with classroom instruction. The recruit is introduced to military customs and courtesies, and Marine Corps history. She studies military justice, defensive measures against nuclear, biological and chemical attacks, first aid, hygiene, Marine Corps personnel administration and regulations governing the wearing of the Marine Corps uniform. Another course helps the new marine improve her grooming and poise.

Like their male counterparts, women marines participate in parades and ceremonies. At Parris Island, recruits learn Marine Corps marching and drill procedures. They practice what they have learned by marching to classes and to meals.

The Marine Corps gives its women recruits 24 hours of formal physical training while they are at Parris Island. In addition, the recruits are encouraged to participate in sports such as volleyball, softball, tennis and bike riding during time set aside for recreation. Before she graduates from recruit training, the new marine must pass a physical fitness test that requires her to meet standards for performing situps, pushups and a timed distance run.

If a recruit, for one reason or another, fails to complete her Parris Island training in the usual eight weeks, she can be moved back to a junior platoon for as much as four weeks of additional training. Most women, however, graduate at the end of eight weeks. No longer green recruits, the graduates leave Parris Island as full-fledged marines, after a colorful graduation ceremony to which parents are invited.

Duty assignments for women marines are determined in

the same way as those for male marines: by aptitude tests taken during recruit training, the preferences of the individual marine and the needs of the Corps. All occupational fields, with the exception of those involving duty with combat forces and a few that require unusual strength, are open to women.

One of the occupational fields to which a woman marine might be assigned is food services. It includes bakers, who make pastry products, bread, ice cream and frozen deserts for Marine dining facilities, and cooks, who prepare and serve food in Marine mess halls. Or she might be assigned as a veterinary technician, responsible for receiving, storing and inspecting food supplies. (Safeguarding food supplies is an important duty of the military veterinarian.) In food services, as in other occupational fields, the woman marine will work side by side with men assigned to the same speciality, and she will be considered for training courses and for promotion on the same basis.

There are several schools to which the Marine Corps sends its food services specialists. The Marine Corps Supply School at Camp Lejeune, North Carolina, trains bakers and offers other courses in the food service field. Veterinary technicians receive their training at Sheppard Air Force Base, in Texas. Cooks can attend the U.S. Army Quartermaster School at Fort Lee, Virginia. Food inspection procedures are taught at the Army Medical Services Veterinary School in Chicago, Illinois.

A recruit who has an aptitude for clerical work might be assigned to the personnel and administration field. In one of the Marine Corps' many offices her duties would include preparing correspondence, maintaining records and files, and perhaps assisting in the interviewing, testing and assignment of other marines. Or she might work in a Marine Corps post office.

Most women marines assigned to the personnel and administration field remain at Parris Island, after graduation from recruit training, to attend a Marine Corps school that will prepare them for their first billet. ("Billet" is the word that marines use when they refer to their job assignment, but it can also mean a marine's living area.)

Marine Corps exchanges are stores in which a wide variety of merchandise is sold to marines and their families. Women marines who are assigned to positions in the exchange system receive their training on the job. A marine may be assigned to an exchange as a bookkeeper. Or her specialist rating may be exchangeman. In that case, her duties would include merchandise control and the supervision of civilian sales personnel. She would learn how to handle sales, how to display merchandise and how to take care of special orders.

Photography offers several career opportunities for the qualified woman marine. She might be assigned as a photographer who operates still cameras, develops film and prints photographs. If she becomes a photojournalist she will work on feature stories for release to both civilian and military newspapers and magazines. As a Marine Corps film editor she would edit motion picture film, catalog completed film and maintain a film library.

Photography specialists are eligible for a number of excellent training courses, among them a 52-week photojournalism course at the University of Syracuse in Syracuse, New

York; a ten-week course in photographic laboratory operation at Fort Monmouth, New Jersey; an eleven-week photographic control course at the Rochester Institute of Technology in New York State; and an eight-week color photo process course at Lowry Air Force Base, Colorado.

Lithography is another career field open to the woman marine who is interested in photography. As a lithographer she will prepare copy for camera work and operate the cameras used in the reproduction process. Marine lithographers also prepare lithographic plates for printing, correct proofs and operate presses and bindery equipment.

In addition to an interest in photography and printing, the marine who wants to be a lithographer should be able to learn quickly. She should also have a good knowledge of spelling, grammar and arithmetic, and the ability to work with machinery.

If a woman marine has had musical training, she is eligible to audition for a Marine Corps assignment that would allow her to use her training. Marine bandsmen play as members of concert bands, marching bands and other musical groups. A marine, whose specialty is field music bugler, sounds the regulation calls and commands on the bugle and performs as a member of a drum and bugle corps. Marines whose specialty is percussion instruments may also be assigned to a drum and bugle corps. Another specialist in the music field is the instrument repairman who inspects, maintains and repairs musical instruments.

The Marine Corps trains its field music buglers at Parris Island or at San Diego, California. Musicians are also sent to the Navy's School of Music at Norfolk, Virginia.

Assigned to the Armed Forces Radio and TV Service on Okinawa, a woman marine sergeant serves as a commentator for the TV program "What's Happening on Okinawa." *(Department of Defense)*

Clerical and mechanical aptitude, combined with the ability to learn quickly and an interest in business technology, could result in an assignment to the career field that the Marine Corps calls data systems. Within that field a woman marine could work with card punch or accounting machines. She could be a computer operator or the programmer who prepares and codes data on various types of computers. Or she could be a data systems librarian who classifies and files magnetic storage devices and makes them available to users.

The Marine Corps' Computer Science School is located at the large Marine base at Quantico, Virginia, on the Potomac River about 35 miles from Washington, D.C. Several courses for data systems specialists are taught at the school.

Quantico is also the location of the school that gives the Marine Corps' woman officer candidates their initial training. Two sessions of the eight-week Woman Officer Candidate Course (WOCC) are held each year—one beginning in June and the other in the fall, usually October.

While she is attending WOCC, an officer candidate lives in a dormitory and shares a room with two or three other candidates. The dormitory buildings have guest lounges, recreation areas and laundry facilities. The candidates eat their meals in a nearby mess hall.

Soon after arrival at Quantico, a candidate receives an issue of Marine Corps uniforms. If she begins her training in the summer, she gets cotton polyester uniforms, two caps, a raincoat, handbag, gloves, scarf and shoes. A candidate who reports in the fall receives the winter uniform issue: the Marine Corps green wool suit, a winter hat, a raincoat, handbag, gloves, scarf and shoes. Before she reports to her first duty assignment, a candidate will receive an allowance for the purchase of additional uniform items.

The woman officer candidate's day begins at 6 A.M. with calisthenics, followed by breakfast. Before reporting to her first class at 9 A.M., she helps ready her dormitory for inspection and prepares to stand inspection herself. The Marine Corps schedules daily inspections to insure that the candidates maintain a high standard of cleanliness and grooming.

Classroom work for the officer candidates includes the study of Marine Corps history, military history, military customs, courtesies and traditions, military law, first aid and good grooming. Some class periods are devoted to panel discussions of current topics. The candidates also study the principles of leadership, and their own potential for leadership is observed by their instructors.

Before she begins her training, an officer candidate must agree to remain at Quantico for at least five weeks. After that time, and until she is commissioned, she can be disenrolled at her own request with no further obligation to the Marine Corps. College graduates who successfully complete the Woman Officer Candidate Course are commissioned second lieutenants in the Marine Corps. After a short vacation, they return to Quantico for the next phase of their training—Basic School.

Women in their junior year of college can apply for training as Marine Corps officer candidates. If they are accepted, they usually attend the Woman Officer Candidate Course during the summer following their junior year. However, they are not commissioned when they finish the course. Instead, they return to college to earn a baccalaureate degree.

They receive their commission when they graduate.

The Marine Corps requires that its college program candidates maintain at least a C average during their final school year, but they need take no military subjects nor participate in military functions.

Financial assistance is available for some college seniors who have successfully completed the Woman Officer Candidate Course. If a student receives assistance, her active duty obligation is increased by six months, to a total of three years.

College students who successfully complete one of the Naval Reserve Officer Training Programs can choose to be commissioned a second lieutenant in the Marine Corps. This option is possible because the Marine Corps is part of the Department of the Navy.

All of the Marine Corps' newly commissioned second lieutenants begin their active military careers with a training course at the Corps' Basic School, located at Quantico's Camp Barrett. The training at Camp Barrett is designed to develop their capabilities as leaders and to prepare them for the duties of Marine Corps company and staff officers. Men and women attend many Basic School classes together.

After a review of subjects studied during their preliminary officer candidate training, Basic School students move on to more advanced courses. The organization and mission of the U.S. Armed Forces, military operations, military supply procedures, military communications and military personnel administration are included in the Basic School curriculum. In addition, women marines attend classes in personal development.

After completing the ten-week Basic School course and

whatever specialty training she might require, the woman marine reports to her first duty assignment. Although she cannot be assigned to a combat-related occupational field, there are many responsible jobs that she can fill. In 1973, 28 of the Marine Corps' 39 occupational fields were available to women, and several others were under consideration for opening to them.

Supply is an occupational field to which many women marine officers are assigned. Within that field, a woman marine can serve as a unit supply officer who is responsible for keeping a Marine Corps unit equipped with whatever it needs to perform its mission. The unit supply officer must see to it that many different kinds of supplies and equipment are ordered, received, stored and issued. She will also arrange for the shipment of government property and the property of marines who are being transferred. And she will maintain records of all the transactions that she handles.

The woman marine who begins her career as a unit supply officer may eventually supervise several supply units. Her title will then be supply officer, and she will be responsible for seeing that Marine Corps supply policies are carried out by the units that she supervises. In addition, she will serve as the commander's adviser on supply matters.

Food services is a career field that offers the woman marine officer many opportunities to use her creative and administrative talents. She may be called upon to prepare menus, supervise the operation of food storage facilities or work out procedures for eliminating waste in the handling of food. Food services officers also inspect kitchens and dining halls, and train food handlers.

Although the fact that they cannot be deployed for combat excludes them from assignment as pilots, women hold other responsible positions in Marine Corps aviation. The woman who is an air traffic control officer supervises the activities of a radar air traffic control center, an air station control tower or some other Marine air traffic control facility. An air traffic control officer is primarily a supervisor, but the marine officer in this career field must be able, when the occasion demands, to take over as controller for approaching and departing aircraft. She will be responsible for the efficient operation of her unit, and for developing and evaluating instrument approach and departure procedures for aircraft using her control facility.

In order to qualify as an air traffic control officer, a woman marine must be certified by the Federal Aviation Administration, and she must meet certain physical requirements.

If she is assigned to a Marine air station as a radar officer, a woman marine will supervise the work of some of the specialists who keep the Marine Corps' radar sets in good working order. As part of her training for a career in this occupational field, she will become familiar with several kinds of radar: course direction radar, air search radar, missile search radar and height finder radar. She will also receive training in the operation of radar beacons and meteorological equipment. In addition to supervising repair work, the radar officer must see to it that repairmen have the tools, test equipment and parts that they need.

Marine Corps intelligence officers supervise the collection of information that might help Marine combat forces carry out their mission. The information comes from photographs, captured documents, prisoners of war and other sources. The woman marine officer assigned to this career field may be called upon to brief marines before a mission and to debrief them at the conclusion of the operation. Her duties may also include instructing combat troops in such subjects as enemy tactics, target recognition, and the characteristics of friendly and enemy ships, aircraft and combat vehicles.

Counterintelligence, which is concerned with keeping valuable information from the enemy, is another function of the intelligence officer. It involves loyalty investigations, censorship, protecting communications and guarding against the activities of spies and saboteurs.

The woman marine who has the ability to master foreign languages, or who already knows a language that the Marine Corps needs, might become a language officer. She could serve as an interpreter in conversations between someone who speaks a foreign language and someone who speaks English, or she could be a translator of material written in a foreign language. In time of war she would use her knowledge of one or more foreign languages to supervise interrogations of enemy soldiers and civilians. She would also examine captured or abandoned war materiel for documents that should be translated into English.

Language officers also translate into a foreign language material that will be used for propaganda purposes, and they teach at Marine Corps language schools.

These are just some of the positions that have attracted young women who were looking for an interesting job that would allow them to make full use of their capabilities. Second Lieutenant Madeline Carroll Davis, explained: "I

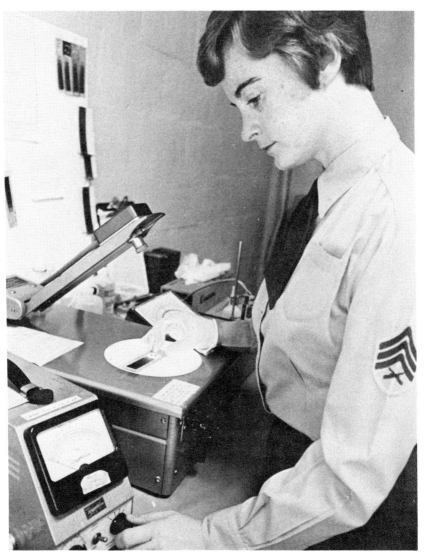

This woman marine is a photographer who spends part of her time in a photographic laboratory developing film and making prints. *(U.S. Marine Corps)*

wanted something challenging and different that would offer me a chance to travel. I wanted a job that would give me the opportunity to explore the unknown, would be character building and would teach me a professional attitude."

Another new woman marine, Second Lieutenant Katherine A. Johnson, said: "I guess the most important reason for joining the Corps was because of the benefits and the opportunity to travel. It also happened to be the best job I could find. Now, I feel a part of the new Corps. I feel I might contribute some new ideas."

Still another reason for becoming a marine was provided by a young black woman, Captain Gloria Smith, who said: "I like being first. Maybe that was one of the major reasons I joined the Marine Corps. I'd heard of black women in the other military branches. However, I had never even seen a woman marine, much less a black woman marine."

During an interview at the Marine Corps' Equal Opportunity Office where she acted as a liaison officer between Congress, the Corps and the enlisted man or woman, Captain Smith remarked that it was no harder for a woman to get ahead in the Corps than in the business world. "Some men think women should not function in an area of responsibility," she said. "I know this is ridiculous and so does almost everybody else. It's a few with this prejudice who make things difficult for the woman with brains and ability."

"We want women who want more than a job," says Colonel Ann Brewer, director of Woman Marines. "We want women with brains who want a chance to use them."

In order to more fully utilize the abilities of its women officers and enlistees, the Marine Corps has revoked or revised regulations that discriminated against women. The Corps no longer restricts women to certain kinds of noncombat positions, and it has discontinued the practice of labeling some positions "for women only." Regulations which limited women officers to command positions that involved primarily the administration of women have been eliminated. These changes mean that women marines serve on an interchangeable basis with men in noncombat occupational fields. And, of course, they have the same opportunities for training and promotion.

# 8

## WOMEN ON
## THE MARCH
## IN THE
## COAST GUARD

 After all but disappearing from that organization at the end of World War II, women are once again being encouraged to join the U.S. Coast Guard. Moreover, both enlisted women and women officers are now eligible for active duty assignments. Formerly, such assignments for women were limited to a few officer positions at Coast Guard Headquarters. Other women who joined the Coast Guard became members of inactive-duty units.

To attract women to its ranks, the Coast Guard has improved their training and job assignments to make opportunities for women as nearly equal to those for men as possible in a seagoing service.

The Coast Guard has opened its Training Center at Cape May, New Jersey, to enlisted women who wish to serve on active duty. Male recruits also report to Cape May for their basic indoctrination. In most respects men and women receive the same training, although they do not train together.

At Cape May, recruits are introduced to the Coast Guard and its missions. They study seamanship, visual signaling and other subjects that will prepare them for service in the Coast Guard. The program for women includes vigorous physical training and hours of drill, including rifle drill.

To be accepted for enlistment for active duty, a woman usually must be qualified to attend a basic petty officer training school when she finishes the course at Cape May. (A petty officer corresponds to the Army's noncommissioned officer.) The petty officer school will prepare her for one of the ratings, or occupational fields, open to her. These ratings include yeoman, storekeeper, hospital corpsman, dental technician and photojournalist. A few women can also become Coast Guard musicians and additional ratings are under consideration for women.

After ten weeks of recruit training at Cape May, the active-duty enlisted woman moves on to the petty officer school to which she has been assigned. There she acquires the theoretical knowledge and practical experience that will help make her a successful member of the Coast Guard.

The woman who becomes a Coast Guard yeoman trains for approximately twelve weeks. Her duties will be clerical in nature and she prepares for them by learning how the Coast Guard handles its letters, messsages and reports. She will also learn how to maintain Coast Guard records and how to operate a variety of office machines. As her skill and experience increase on the job, she will be given more responsibility, and perhaps more training, until she becomes the equivalent of an office manager.

Coast Guard storekeepers have duties similar to those of an accountant in a civilian business. An experienced storekeeper's responsibilities will include processing payrolls, making payments and keeping financial records. Storekeepers order, receive, store and issue the supplies that the Coast Guard needs to perform its missions. They also keep records to insure that supplies and equipment are available when and where they are needed.

Storekeepers receive twelve weeks of special training.

The enlisted woman who becomes a hospital corpsman trains for sixteen weeks before reporting to one of the Coast Guard's shore stations, where she will assist professional medical personnel. She may be assigned to ward or operating room duties, or she may serve as a technician in such fields as X ray, pharmacy or epidemiology.

Dental technicians, who also receive sixteen weeks of training, perform dental, clinical and administrative duties for dental officers. Some Coast Guard dental technicians work with mobile dental clinics, which make periodic visits to the service's smaller stations.

The enlisted woman who becomes a photojournalist will prepare the news releases that keep coast guardsmen and the general public informed about Coast Guard developments. A photojournalist's duties may include working on TV and radio scripts, taking photographs and editing newspapers and other publications.

Photojournalists receive their training in military journalism schools.

At the conclusion of their training at basic petty officer school, Coast Guard enlisted women report to their first duty stations. Because they cannot be assigned aboard ships or aircraft or to an isolated post, the duty stations most probably will be at a Coast Guard base, depot or school. Wherever they are assigned, the women will have the same opportunities for advanced training and promotions as their male counterparts. And they will receive the same pay and benefits as men of equal rank.

For the young woman who wishes to be a part of the Coast Guard, but not on a full-time basis, there is an expanded inactive-duty program. The woman who enlists in this program attends a two-week indoctrination course and fulfills the remainder of her service obligation as a member of a Coast Guard Reserve unit. She trains with her unit on one weekend a month, for which she receives four days' pay. In addition, she participates in two consecutive weeks of training each year. Her pay is the same as that received by male members of the unit who hold a similar rating, and she is considered for promotion on an equal basis. She can improve her chances for promotion by taking advantage of Coast Guard training courses.

If a national emergency should require the Coast Guard to expand its strengh, the inactive-duty woman would be called to active duty. She could be assigned to a Coast Guard station to fill a vacancy in her rating, or she might be assigned to use her skill and training in preparing recruits for service with the Coast Guard.

The woman most apt to be accepted for enlistment in the inactive-duty program has a civilian skill that the Coast

At the Coast Guard's Officer Candidate School at Yorktown, Virginia, a woman candidate learns to dismantle and reassemble small arms. *(U.S. Coast Guard)*

Guard can use. Depending upon her skill, she enters the program as a third, second or first class petty officer. The enlistee begins her association with the Coast Guard at the Reserve Training Center at Yorktown, Virginia, where she attends the Reserve Enlisted Basic Indoctrination (REBI) School. Men with certain civilian skills, but no previous military training, also attend REBI School. Courses at REBI School prepare enlistees for service with their local Coast Guard Reserve training unit by introducing them to the Coast Guard way of doing things.

Formerly restricted to the yeoman and storekeeper ratings, inactive-duty enlisted women can now choose from eleven occupational fields, with the prospect that the number will increase. In addition to the yeoman, storekeeper, hospital corpsman, dental technician and photojournalist ratings that are also open to active-duty enlisted women, Coast Guard women in the inactive Reserve are eligible for the ratings of boatswain's (pronounced bosun's) mate, port securityman, engineman, radioman, subsistence specialist and data processing technician.

Coast Guard boatswain's mates fill positions on all of the service's ships and at most shore stations. However, the woman who receives a boatswain's mate rating would probably receive most of her training ashore, at least initially. She will acquire a knowledge of seamanship and become familiar with such terms as rigging, hauser, winch, tackle and cargo net. The use of signal flags, lights and navigation instruments will also be included in her training. She will learn how cargo should be handled and stored and the procedures for maintaining Coast Guard ships and boats.

The Coast Guard is the federal agency responsible for all aspects of security in United States ports, including the safe handling, transportation and storage of explosives and other dangerous cargoes. Coast Guardsmen who work in this field are called port securitymen. The woman reservist who becomes a port securityman must be familiar with the regulations covering the security of vessels, harbors and waterfront facilities and with the equipment that the Coast Guard uses in carrying out its port security mission.

If she receives the rating of engineman, the enlisted reservist will learn to operate and repair the various kinds of

A woman officer candidate and her male classmates hang on to the lines in a lifeboat being lowered from the Coast Guard training ship *Unimak*. *(U.S. Coast Guard)*

internal combustion engines used in Coast Guard ships and boats. The engineman must know how to use tools and precision measuring instruments and how to prepare reports and keep work records.

Coast Guard radiomen operate radios, radio direction finders, teletypewriters and facsimile equipment. They adjust and repair this equipment, and teach others how to use and repair it. The woman who holds a radioman rating will also learn how to transmit and receive messages in the International Morse Code.

The training of the inactive-duty reservist who is a subsistence specialist will include preparing menus, keeping cost accounts, ordering provisions, and receiving and storing them. She will also learn how food is prepared and served in Coast Guard dining halls.

When the woman who becomes a data processing technician in the Coast Guard Reserve reports for a training session, she will work with the service's electronic accounting equipment. In addition to operating the equipment, her duties could include designing card layouts and report forms, programming and acting as an office manager.

At the same time that it inaugurated new programs for enlisted women, the Coast Guard opened its formerly all-male Officer Candidate School to women. The school, located at Yorktown, Virginia, offers seventeen weeks of instruction in such subjects as navigation, seamanship, communications and the principles of effective leadership.

At Yorktown, women attend classes with male officer candidates. When the women graduate as ensigns, the Coast Guard considers special qualifications, personal preferences and the needs of the service in making their active-duty assignments, just as it does with its men graduates. Women officers are assigned to all Coast Guard mission areas, except those that require duty on operational aircraft and vessels or duty at isolated stations. They are eligible for posts that involve commanding men as well as women.

Newly commissioned ensigns in the Coast Guard's Women's Reserve have an initial active-duty obligation of three years. They can retain their Reserve status if they wish, or they can apply for integration into the Coast Guard's Regular, or permanent, force. In the latter case, they are eligible for the 30-year Coast Guard careers that are available to men.

Many of the Coast Guard's women enlistees and officers favor dropping the acronym SPAR. They point out that *Semper Paratus* and its translation, Always Ready, apply to all Coast Guard personnel, not just to women. Moreover, the women, who serve on an equal basis with men, feel that the acronym sets them apart from other members of the Coast Guard.

# 9

## PROFESSIONAL
## OPPORTUNITIES
## IN THE
## MILITARY HEALTH
## FIELDS

Because each of the armed services provides medical care for its members and their families, military nursing and other military health fields offer many well-paid career opportunities. The woman who becomes a military nurse, doctor, dentist, dietician, physical therapist or occupational therapist will enter her chosen service as an officer; therefore, she must be able to meet requirements for commissioning as well as the certification requirements of her profession.

Medical care officers belong to a special department of their military service. In the Air Force, it is the Air Force Medical Service. The Army has a Medical Department. The Navy, which supplies medical officers to the Marine Corps, has a Bureau of Medicine and Surgery. The medical departments are organized into corps, usually a nursing corps, a medical corps, a dental corps and a medical service corps. The woman member of one of these corps is not a WAC officer, nor is she a Waf or a Wave. Rather, depending on her service, she is a member of the Army Nurse Corps, the Air Force Nurse Corps, the Navy Nurse Corps or of one of the other medical specialist corps.

In 1973, the Air Force had 3,500 women officers in the medical care field; the Army had 3,200; and the Navy, 2,214. Approximately 85 percent of these women were nurses.

The mission that the Air Force has assigned to its nurses also applies to the Army and Navy Nurse Corps. It is: to provide the most efficient nursing care in a wide variety of specialties; to teach patients and their families the principles of personal health; to teach and supervise nonprofessional personnel in nursing care assignments; and to participate in research activities.

In general, military nurses have the same duties as civilian nurses. There are some differences between military and civilian nursing, however. The military nurse is an officer of the Armed Forces who receives the pay and privileges of her rank. Her take-home pay is very likely higher than it would be if she were a civilian nurse. In addition, she receives free medical and dental care, she is entitled to shop at military exchanges and commissaries where prices are lower and, if she lives off-post, she receives a housing allowance.

Most military nurses consider their opportunities for advancement to positions of authority, such as head nurse, to be greater than in civilian nursing. They also feel that they work more closely with doctors than would be the case in a civilian hospital. "We work as a team here. The doctors

In 1918, when this photo was taken, 1,386 women were wearing the scarlet-lined, dark blue cape and the wide-brimmed hat of the Navy nurse. *(U.S. Navy)*

One of the Army's nurse-midwives counsels a new mother. Nurse-midwives have taken over some of the duties once performed by doctors. *(U.S. Army)*

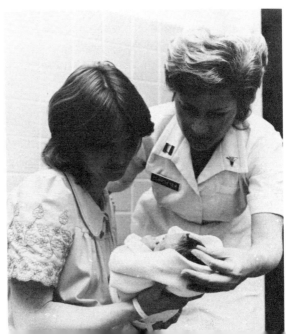

depend on you more and expect you to do more, " is the way one Army nurse put it.

Like other military officers, nurses are eligible for promotion after specified periods of service. In the Air Force and the Army they can be promoted up to the rank of brigadier general, and in the Navy to the corresponding rank of rear admiral.

When a registered nurse joins the Air Force Nurse Corps, she receives her introduction to military life and military nursing at Sheppard Air Force Base, Texas. After completing the orientation course at Sheppard, she reports to her first duty assignment, usually at an Air Force hospital in the United States. She may be assigned to general staff nursing, where the demand for nurses is greatest, or to a nursing specialty. Later assignments could take her to Air Force health facilities in Germany, England, Japan, Greenland, Spain, Greece, Newfoundland, the Azores, the Canal Zone, Puerto Rico, Okinawa, Italy, Hawaii, Turkey, the Philippines, South Korea or Southeast Asia.

One of the most important advantages that the military nurse enjoys is the opportunity to obtain professional education and training at government expense. Air Force nurses attend workshops in their specialties at civilian institutions. They can also volunteer for training in three special Air Force nursing fields: flight nursing, aerospace nursing and nurse-midwifery.

Air Force flight nurses assist in the evacuation of patients by air to a facility where adequate medical treatment is available. The flight nurse, who must be medically acceptable for flying, prepares for her specialty by attending a six-week course taught at the School of Aerospace Medicine at Brooks Air Force Base, San Antonio, Texas. She studies aviation physiology, psychology, in-flight care of patients and therapeutics. When she completes the course, she adds silver wings to her uniform insignia and reports for medical evacuation duty that will take her to every part of the world.

While she and her patients are airborne, the flight nurse is responsible for their medical welfare. To keep current in the latest nursing procedures, she returns to hospital duty between tours of aeromedical evacuation duty.

The Air Force's School of Aerospace Medicine also trains nurses who want to specialize in preventive medicine. To qualify for the one-year aerospace medicine course, an Air Force nurse must have a baccalaureate degree and three years' experience as an Air Force nurse. She must also have completed flight nurse training and be physically qualified for flying duty.

Air Force nurse-midwives free busy doctors for other duties by caring for selected maternity patients. The nurse-midwife counsels expectant mothers, delivers babies and evaluates newborn infants. The nurse who has at least two years' experience in the maternity nursing field is eligible for nurse-midwifery training.

If an Air Force nurse has completed all but one year or less of the work required for a bachelor's or a master's degree in nursing, the Air Force has a program called Operation Bootstrap which will allow her to attend an accredited college or university to earn that degree. The Air Force Institute of Technology offers courses leading to a bachelor's or master's degree in nursing, which a nurse can also take while she retains her active-duty status. And the U.S. Armed Forces Institute and the Air University offer extension courses in health-related subjects.

Like the Air Force, the Army offers the members of its Nurse Corps many opportunities for professional advancement. In addition, the Army will provide financial assistance to qualified men and women who wish to become nurses, and to registered nurses who have returned to school to obtain a bachelor's or a master's degree in nursing. Students who receive assistance agree to serve in the Army Nurse Corps after they graduate.

Students enrolled in an Army-approved hospital school of nursing are eligible for 12 months of financial assistance. Students enrolled in an Army-approved college or university school of nursing can receive up to 24 months of assistance. The woman who takes advantage of either one of these programs enlists in the Army as a private first class. Although she has no military duties, she receives a private first class's pay and allowances. If she is in the baccalaureate degree program, the Army also pays for her tuition, books and fees.

Students who receive financial assistance for twelve months or less agree to serve for at least two years as a commissioned officer in the Army Nurse Corps. Those who participate for 13 to 24 months agree to serve for three years.

Another Army plan offers a full four years of assistance to nursing students who are accepted as Army Nurse Corps candidates. A young woman in this program enlists in the Army as a private third class, and spends two years in a college or university of her choice. The school must be approved by the Army, however. The student receives the pay and allowances of her grade, and the Army takes care of her tuition and some of her fees. She has no military duties. After two years, the Army Nurse Corps candidate enrolls in the University of Maryland School of Nursing to complete work for a nursing degree. She lives and attends classes at the Army's Walter Reed Medical Center in Washington, D.C., where her education and training are directed by University of Maryland School of Nursing faculty members.

When she graduates, the Army Nurse Corps candidate is commissioned a first lieutenant in the Army Nurse Corps. She must serve a minimum of three years on active duty.

The Army's Registered Nurse Student Program is open to registered nurses who are within 24 months of receiving a bachelor's or master's degree in nursing. To qualify, a nurse must be a full-time student, or accepted as a student, at an Army-approved college or university school of nursing. She is commissioned an officer in the Army Nurse Corps and receives the salary of her rank. As is the case with the other programs, the Registered Nurse Student Program requires no military duties until a student receives her degree. Participants who received assistance for 12 months or less agree to serve in the Army Nurse Corps for two years after graduation. Those who are in the program from 12 to 24 months agree to serve for three years.

All Army nurses begin their military service with six weeks at Medical Field Service School, a part of Brooke Army Medical Center at Fort Sam Houston, San Antonio, Texas. Lectures, films, conferences and demonstrations introduce the new medical officers to the Army and the Army Nurse Corps. A few days in a simulated field support hospital prepare them for possible duty in a combat area. An Army nurse's first assignment will take her to an Army hospital in the United States, or to an overseas area where vacancies exist. The Army has medical facilities in France, Germany, Italy, Japan, Korea, Okinawa, Ethiopia and Southeast Asia.

Like other military nurses, the Army nurse has many opportunities to continue her education. If she wishes to specialize, she can take courses that the Army offers at its hospitals. Operating room nursing, anesthesiology, maternal and child care nursing, psychiatric nursing and intensive care nursing are some of the areas in which an Army nurse can specialize. With the exception of operating room nursing, the courses usually obligate the nurse to extend her commitment to serve in the Army by the length of time spent in the course.

Short courses, lasting one or two weeks, are also available to the Army nurse. These courses do not require her to extend her service obligation.

Each year, a number of the Army's registered nurses who have decided to make Army nursing their career return to school to earn an undergraduate or graduate degree in nursing. The Army continues their pay and allowances while they spend up to a full year in school.

Newly commissioned Navy nurses receive their introduction to the naval establishment at the Newport Officer Training Center. During a four-week officer indoctrination course, they acquire basic information about the Navy and its Bureau of Medicine and Surgery. They also learn what their rights and responsibilities will be as naval officers. Their introduction to Navy nursing comes when they report to their first duty assignment.

The National Naval Medical Center, which includes a large hospital, is in Bethesda, Maryland. Other Navy hospitals and medical facilities are located at naval bases throughout the United States, and in several foreign countries. In addition, the Navy nurse may have an opportunity to serve aboard a hospital ship. During the Vietnam conflict two such ships, the U.S.S. *Sanctuary* and the U.S.S. *Repose* operated off the Vietnamese coast.

Several fields of specialization are open to the Navy nurse. She may be an anesthetist nurse, a flight nurse, a public health nurse, a neuropsychiatric nurse, an obstetrical nurse, a pediatrics nurse, an operating room nurse, an orthopedic nurse, a nursing instructor, a nursing service administrator, a charge nurse or a research nurse. Moreover, the Navy's Nurse Corps Officer Education Program will help her prepare for her chosen specialty.

Full-time instruction, in a civilian college or university, is available to the Navy nurse who wants to study for an undergraduate or a graduate degree in nursing service administration, nursing education, nursing research, supervision and in several clinical specialties. Navy nurses who wish to become anesthetists study for one year at George Washington University in Washington, D.C., and at the Naval Medical School in nearby Bethesda, Maryland. This is followed by a year of clinical experience, under instruction, at a naval hospital. Operating room and orthopedic nurses receive their special training at a naval hospital. The Navy also sends nurses to a course in Navy management offered by the Naval

Postgraduate School in Monterey, California. The course leads to a master of science degree.

Undergraduate student nurses are the beneficiaries of several plans providing for financial assistance from the Navy. The Nurse Corps Candidate Program provides up to two years of paid education for student nurses attending an approved college or university school of nursing. Students enter the program as officer candidate hospitalmen and receive the pay of that grade, although they have no military duties. In addition, the Navy takes care of tuition, fees and textbook expenses. When they graduate, the candidates are commissioned ensigns in the Navy Nurse Corps. Graduates who received financial assistance for one year are obligated to serve for two years in the Navy Nurse Corps. Two years of assistance requires three years of active duty.

Nursing students enrolled in an accredited hospital school of nursing are eligible for Navy scholarships during their senior year. Scholarship holders receive the base pay and allowances of a naval hospitalman, and they become ensigns in the Navy Nurse Corps when they graduate. Their service obligation is two years.

Registered nurses who become Nurse Corps candidates, while attending an accredited school of anesthesia, receive the pay and allowances of a Navy ensign for twelve months prior to graduation. The candidates perform no military duties, but they do agree to serve in the Navy Nurse Corps for two years.

Men and women who are serving in the Navy as hospital corpsmen are eligible for the Navy's Enlisted Nursing Education Program. Participants become officer candidates and receive the base pay and allowances of that grade while they study for a baccalaureate degree at an approved school of nursing. The Navy takes care of tuition, fees and textbook expenses. Upon graduation the students are commissioned ensigns in the Navy Nurse Corps. In return for the Navy's assistance, students in the Enlisted Nursing Education Program agree to serve four years on active duty.

Nursing is only one of the military medical and health career fields that offer unusual opportunities for education and advancement. The Air Force, the Army and the Navy also have programs that provide financial assistance to young people who are preparing for careers as doctors, dentists, dieticians, physical therapists and occupational therapists. The woman in one of these programs assumes an active-duty obligation that varies with the amount of assistance she receives. And, like the military nurse, she can continue her professional education while she is serving on active duty.

In addition to the educational opportunities which are available to her, the military woman in one of the medical and health career fields finds, in most cases, that her officer's pay and allowances amount to more than the salary she could earn as a civilian. Moreover, military promotions bring an automatic increase in salary. And she will compete for promotion and for positions of increased responsibility on an equal basis with the men in her career field.

# 10

## "REGARDLESS OF RACE, SEX, CREED OR NATIONAL ORIGIN"

As the Department of Defense continues with its efforts to make military service a model of equal opportunity "regardless of race, sex, creed or national origin," what do women think about the opportunities open to them when they join the Armed Forces?

Lieutenant Janette E. Baralli's Air Force assignments have included a tour of duty at the North American Air Defense Command's Space Defense Center, in the Colorado Rockies, where she kept track of the data generated by a worldwide network of satellite tracking stations. When asked for her opinion about career opportunities for Air Force women, Lieutenant Baralli said: "In comparison with civilian jobs, we've got it made. I expect women in the Air Force will be pilots within a year, then astronaut training will follow."

Meanwhile, the commander of the Space Defense Center expressed satisfaction with the performance of Lieutenant Baralli and other women assigned to the Center. "They have shown that they can be very capable crew members," he said. "Women have been able to blend into what was formerly a male-dominated field, and the mixed manning has not created any conflicts or difficulties whatsoever. Women perform their functions on a par with men in the Space Defense Center. We have Wafs who are working in space surveillance, missile warning, computers, as analysts and in other jobs associated with satellite detection and tracking programs."

In explaining why she joined the Air Force, Second Lieutenant Blythe Fairfull, who graduated from Colorado State University with a degree in chemistry, said: "The Air Force looked like a good opportunity. In civilian life a graduate chemist finds there is either too much education, or not enough experience to get a good job. I wanted a chance to use my education and the Air Force offered it. I think it was a wise choice."

The Air Force sent Lieutenant Fairfull to its Fuel Management Officer School. When she graduated, she put her knowledge of chemistry to work as a fuels management officer at one of the bases where Air Force pilots receive their training. Her duties included running laboratory tests on airplane fuel before it went into storage tanks, and again when the fuel was needed for aircraft operations.

Captain Lorraine Potter, the first woman chaplain to join the Air Force, couldn't obtain the pastoral experience she wanted in the civilian world. "They would accept me as Lorraine Potter," she said, "but not as a pastor. I made

Lieutenant Janette E. Baralli poses with a map indicating the paths of satellites tracked by the North American Air Defense Command's Space Defense Center. *(U.S. Air Force)*

headway, but they would not consider me to preach full time."

In the Air Force, she hoped to have an opportunity to do clinical pastoral work in addition to her regular duties as a military chaplain.

Captain Marcelite C. Jordan trained at an Air Force maintenance school for her job as the maintenance officer of an American fighter squadron based in Thailand. Speaking of her assignment to a position that was once closed to women, Captain Jordan said: "I believe women can do any job outside those requiring heavy physical work, although there are women capable of even that. Being a woman should not immediately eliminate you. Intelligence really rules the world." She added: "I want to stay on the flight line, but that doesn't exclude me from trying other things."

The first WAF officer to be assigned as the commander of a nearly all-male air base group was interested only in the opportunity to do a good job. Colonel Norma Brown said: "I have no desire for notoriety as the first woman commander to make good as the commander of a male unit. I simply want to earn a reputation as a good group commander, period!" Of her ambition to become the commander of an Air Force base she said: "If at a later time I have the opportunity to become a base commander, then I want to be the best at that job that I possibly can be."

Captain Maxine (Micki) King is proud of the gold medal she won in the three-meter diving competition at the 1972 Summer Olympic Games in Munich, Germany. She is also proud of her Air Force career, which has included an assignment to the Air Force Academy as an administrative officer. "The Air Force offered me an interesting, challenging career and at the same time, it gives me an opportunity to pursue my diving career," she said.

When the Army assigned Wacs to its Drill Sergeant School for the first time, the women participated in the same program as male students, with only minor changes to reflect the differences between men's and women's physical training. One of the women students, who would soon be training WAC recruits, expressed her approval of the decision to open the school to women: "I feel this is a good sign for the future of the WAC," she said. "After finishing this school, we will be better trained and informed."

Lieutenant Junior Grade (LTJG) Judith Ann Neuffer was

serving with the Navy's Combat Direction System Support Activity in San Diego, California, when she heard that the Navy had opened its flight training to a limited number of women. She applied and was the first candidate to be accepted. "I've grown up with flying," she explained. "It's practically second nature to me, and when I saw I had an opportunity to do something I really love to do in the Navy, immediately I decided to try."

The Navy sent LTJG Edna Vance to Fleet Intelligence School at Norfolk, Virginia, when she finished Officer Candidate School. Then she reported for duty at the Fleet Intelligence Center at Jacksonville, Florida.

"My Jacksonville assignment was really challenging," she recalled a few years later. "I was top-secret control officer, responsible for the security of all top-secret material at the Jacksonville command. That was a lot of responsibility for a young woman recently out of college. But a responsible position was what I was looking for when I joined the Navy."

Lieutenant Ann Girouard, a lawyer, joined the Navy "because I thought it would be good legal training. Besides, the Navy allows me to travel."

Lieutenant Girouard encountered little bias against women lawyers in the course of her legal work in the Navy. "I think clients will accept you as a competent attorney if you fulfill your duties with competence," she said.

Navy Airman Roseann Roberts, who wanted to work in the formerly all-male field of aviation electronics, achieved her ambition with the help of Navy training courses. She became interested in aviation electronics at her first duty station. "Although I was a seaman at the time, teaching Morse code, I was working around aviation," she recalled. "I guess that is where I first began to like it."

Roseann's application for electronics training was approved, and she spent 36 weeks at the Naval Training Center at Great Lakes, Illinois. During the remainder of her enlistment she worked in an electronics shop.

Upon completing her enlistment, Roseann left the Navy, but she continued to work in electronics. After seven years as a civilian, however, Roseann rejoined the Navy. "I felt sure I could stay in the electronics field and hoped I could get into aviation electronics," she said.

"I was a bit shocked when she asked to work in aviation electronics," recalled the commander of the squadron to which Airman Roberts was assigned. "But she has proved herself to be thoroughly capable in the electronics field. I'm all for qualified people, be they men or women, doing the job they like best."

Not only did Airman Roberts receive the coveted assignment to aviation electronics, but she became the Navy's first female plane captain as well. Every Navy electronics technician must first qualify as a plane captain, a technician who is responsible for the maintenance of a particular aircraft. In Airman Roberts' case, the aircraft was a helicopter, and she enrolled in a three-month helicopter plane captain course. She learned how to refuel a helicopter, how to perform maintenance checks and how to use hand signals to relay instructions to pilots.

At the ceremony that marked her graduation from the plane captain course, Airman Roberts said: "It's just great.

I've always wanted to work in aviation and for me this is a dream come true."

Someday Roseann would like to fly as a member of a helicopter crew. "But that's in the future," she says. "Right now I'm happy doing what I like best, working in aviation electronics."

Another Wave with a successful career in naval aviation is Master Chief Air Controlman Lue L. Haas who became leading chief of air operations at Cecil Field, Florida. With 220 people under her direction, Chief Haas was responsible for coordinating all air activities at Cecil Field. Earlier in her career, Chief Haas had been the first woman to graduate from the Navy's advanced ground control school.

When asked if she would recommend a Navy career to other women, Chief Haas replied: "Yes, but a woman should first decide what she wants for herself. It will never hurt her, and she will mature and benefit from experiences and educational advantages the Navy offers."

A Wave stationed on Guam, in the western Pacific Ocean, would have agreed with Chief Haas. Of her career as a Navy photographer, she said: "It's a lot more challenging than being a secretary in some nondescript office building."

Speaking of her assignment as special projects officer for the director of Women Marines, Lieutenant Linda C. White said: "The Marine Corps draws out the personality and talents in each one of us. It's because we are given so much responsibility. When I arrived here, I was assigned the job of writing a new curriculum for the officers' training program and designing a mess dress [a uniform worn on formal or ceremonial occasions] for enlisted women. Wow, that was too much! I'm only a first lieutenant."

Marine Lieutenant Katy Wright, a systems analyst, was equally enthusiastic about her work with computers. "Computer programming gives you a chance to be an individual, to make changes in the existing programs, to introduce a fresh, new idea," she said. "You're not limited to reconstructing what other people are doing with the computer."

Major Patricia Hook had this to say, about her assignment as a Marine Corps public affairs officer, "Keeping marines in the public eye, making the public sensitive to them and their activities—it's quite a job. If there's a marine doing outstanding work, I'll have a picture taken, a film clip made or release a story. It's a public relations job, and something new and interesting comes up every day."

One of seven women marines assigned to Cherry Point Marine Air Station, North Carolina, as training device technicians and instructors, Lance Corporal Sally Ashland used an F-4J cockpit simulator to teach fighter pilots how to handle aircraft emergencies. About her work she said: "The training really does help pilots when they are flying and one of these emergencies does happen. They'll know then how to react and won't make a serious mistake."

Lance Corporal Ashland prepared for her job at Cherry Point, and for a career in aviation, with study at the Navy's Avionics Technician School. "To get this job I attended twenty weeks of training at avionics school," she said. "It took me a year to get my present MOS [military occupational specialty]. It is really a neat job. I will, hopefully, get a backseat pilot's license myself someday."

Using the controls of her F–4 trainer, Lance Corporal Sally Ashland sets up a problem for a marine pilot in the simulated F–4 cockpit at her left. *(U.S. Marine Corps)*

Sally, and the other women marine training device instructors at the Cherry Point Marine Air Station, earned the praise of their supervisor, George Rice. "Women make outstanding aviation instructors," he said. "First, they are highly motivated. They have set goals for themselves in learning a profession. They are psychologically suited for the close attention required. And they take a great deal of pride in their jobs."

In addition to the satisfaction that they get from the career opportunities that are available to them, women in the Armed Forces enjoy other benefits as well.

Frequent pay increases keep military salaries on a par with those paid in civilian life. Moreover, there are extra allowances for housing and food, for dependents and for uniforms. Medical and dental care are provided by the government, along with medical care for dependents. There are no deductions from paychecks for this care, although social security payments are deducted. Low-cost life insurance, commissary and base exchange privileges help the serviceman and servicewomen stretch their dollars. Women enjoy all of these benefits on an equal basis with men.

Travel is another benefit enjoyed by the military woman. Because their country's commitments are worldwide, American servicemen and servicewomen who wish to work in a foreign country are often able to do so. Thirty days of leave, with pay, each year insures everyone an opportunity to travel. In some cases the travel can be done free of charge on military space-available flights and scheduled airlines offer reduced fares to service personnel.

Retirement provisions for military women are the same as those for men. After 20 years of service, a woman who retires receives 50 percent of her monthly basic pay at the time of retirement. After 30 years of service, she receives 75 percent of her monthly basic pay.

A servicewoman who retires or successfully completes her enlistment is eligible, under the GI bill, for 36 months of financial assistance while she attends a college or training school. (She can also use the GI bill for college expenses while on active duty.) She is eligible for Veterans Administration and Federal Housing Administration housing loans (also available to the woman on active duty).

The Reserve programs of the Armed Forces are open to the woman who does not wish to serve the usual four to six years on active duty. A woman in one of these programs acquires basic military and vocational skills during a brief period of active duty. She then returns home to participate in Reserve training during the remainder of her service obligation. On one weekend a month, or one evening a week, plus two weeks each summer, she will be improving her skills, winning military promotions and earning extra income just as the men in her Reserve unit do. She will also acquire credit toward a Reserve retirement.

Another benefit of a military career that women share equally with men is the knowledge that they are serving their country. Moreover, there is no question but what their services are needed if the United States is to maintain an adequate military force of volunteers.

In a 1973 speech to the Defense Advisory Committee on Women in the Services, Secretary of Defense Elliott P. Richardson spoke for the Department of Defense when he said: "We need to make more and better use of women. We say this not just because we're for, in principle, the idea of assuring equality of opportunity to women. We're not talking about the Department of Defense or the services as instruments for putting an end to the vestiges of discrimination toward women. We're talking about the very direct interests of the services, for their own purposes, in doing a better job for the United States in the era of the All-Volunteer Force." The secretary added: "We're not thinking in terms of what we can do for women, we're thinking in terms of what women can do for us and for national security. And I'm not sure that we are asking them to do enough."

Women are on the march in the Armed Forces. They are moving into formerly "men-only" jobs and proving that they are capable of handling them. And in the Air Force, the Army, the Navy, the Marine Corps and the Coast Guard women are finding an equality of opportunity denied them in many civilian careers.

# INDEX

Administrative careers:
in the Army, 80, 88
in the Coast Guard, 127–28
in the Marine Corps, 113–14
in the Navy, 99, 108
All-Volunteer Force, 45–46
Amazons, 24
Aptitude tests, for recruits, 50
Army-Navy Nurse Act, 44, 45
Auxiliaries, in British military
forces, 35
Aviation careers:
in the Army, 79
in the Marine Corps, 121,
153–54
in the Navy, 96–97, 102, 109,
149–50, 150–52

Bailey, Mildred C., 91
Basic training:
in the Air Force, 54–59
in the Army, 74–77
in the Coast Guard, 126–27
in the Marine Corps, 110–
12
in the Navy, 92–94
Benefits, of military service,
154–55, 156
Boadicea, 25–26
Boatswain's mates, 131
Bobbitt, Billie M., 58

Brewer, Ann, 124
Brewer, Lucy, 32

Civil War:
nurses in, 34–35
women in, 32–35
Computer specialists:
in the Air Force, 70
in the Navy, 153
Confederate Army, women in,
32–34

Dahomey, women warriors of,
25
Data systems specialists:
in the Coast Guard, 133
in the Marine Corps, 117
Defense, Department of, 17–19
Dental technicians:
in the Coast Guard, 128
in the Navy, 99–100
Divers, in the Navy, 100–101

Education and training officers,
in the Air Force, 72
Electricians, in the Air Force,
61–62
Electronics technicians, in the
Navy, 98, 150–52
Engineers:
civil, in the Navy, 108

development, in the Air Force, 72
Exchange specialists, in the Marine Corps, 114

Financial assistance:
in the Air Force Nurse Corps, 139
in the Army Nurse Corps, 140–41, 142
in the Navy Nurse Corps, 143–45
Food service specialists:
in the Coast Guard, 133
in the Marine Corps, 113, 120

Hays, Anna Mae, 9–12
Army career of, 10–12
promotion to brigadier general of, 9–10
Helicopter mechanics, in the Air Force, 63–64
Hoisington, Elizabeth P., 16–17
Army career of, 12, 14–15
promotion to brigadier general of, 9–10
"Human Goals," 46–47

Information officers:
in the Army, 88
in the Marine Corps, 153
Intelligence officers:
in the Air Force, 69–70
in the Army, 87
in the Marine Corps, 121–22
in the Navy, 150

Joan of Arc, 26–28

Language specialists:
in the Army, 79
in the Marine Corps, 122
Law enforcement specialists, in the Air Force, 65
Legal officers, in the Navy, 107, 150
Lithography specialists, in the Marine Corps, 115

Marinettes, 36–37
Medical care, military careers in, 135–45
in the Army, 79
in the Coast Guard, 128
Musicians:
in the Army, 79
in the Marine Corps, 115
in the Navy, 100

Nurses:
in the Civil War, 34–35
in the Spanish-American War, 35

Oath of enlistment, 51–52
Officer candidate training:
in the Air Force, 66–69
in the Army, 80–86
in the Coast Guard, 133
in the Marine Corps, 117–19
in the Navy, 102–6

Personnel officers:
in the Army, 88
in the Navy, 108
Photography specialists:
in the Army, 79–80
in the Marine Corps, 114–15
Photojournalist specialists, in the Coast Guard, 128

Pitcher, Molly, 29–32
Promotion restrictions, for women, 15–16, 17
Protective equipment specialists, in the Air Force, 60–61

Radio operators:
  in the Air Force, 62–63
  in the Coast Guard, 133
  in the Navy, 98–99
Recruiters, 47–48, 50
  addresses of, 49f.
  in the Army, 80, 87
Requirements:
  for commissioning, 50, 52–53
  for enlistment, 50, 51
Reserve programs, 155–56
  in the Coast Guard, 129–33
Resor, Stanley R., 10
Restricted assignments:
  in the Air Force, 59, 69
  in the Army, 77, 79
  in the Coast Guard, 129, 134
  in the Marine Corps, 110, 113, 120, 121, 125
  in the Navy, 94, 96, 107
Revolutionary War, women in, 28–32
Richardson, Elliott P., 156
Rogers, Edith N., 38

Sampson, Deborah, 28–29
*Sanctuary*, Waves assigned to, 94, 96, 102
Scholarships:
  Air Force ROTC, 68
  Army ROTC, 83–84
  Navy ROTC, 105–6
  (*see also* Financial assistance)
Scientific careers, in the Air Force, 70, 147
Spanish-American War, nurses in, 35
SPAR (U.S. Coast Guard Women's Reserve), in World War II, 38, 41–42, 43
  (*see also* U.S. Coast Guard, women in)
Storekeepers, in the Coast Guard, 128
Supply officers:
  in the Marine Corps, 120
  in the Navy, 107–8

Training devices specialists:
  in the Air Force, 64–65
  in the Marine Corps, 153–54
  in the Navy, 97–98

Uniforms:
  of enlisted Wacs, 75
  of enlisted Wafs, 55–56
  of enlisted Waves, 93
  of enlisted women marines, 111
  of WAC officers, 81
  of WAF officers, 67
  of WAVE officers, 105
  of women marine officers, 117–18
U.S. Air Force, 19
  Nurse Corps, 136, 138–39
  Reserve Officer Training Corps, 66, 68–69
  (*see also* WAF)
U.S. Army, 9–10, 19–21, 86
  Nurse Corps, 35, 36, 37, 44, 139–42
  Reserve Officer Training Corps, 82–84
  (*see also* WAC)

U.S. Coast Guard, 22–23
women in, 126–34
basic training of, 126–27, 130
in the Coast Guard Reserve, 129–33
enlisted specialties of, 127–28, 130–33
officer candidate training of, 133
officer specialties of, 133–34
(*see also* SPAR)
U.S. Marine Corps, 22
Women's Reserve, in World War II, 38, 40–41, 42–43
(*see also* Women Marines)
U.S. Navy, 21
Nurse Corps, 35, 36, 37, 44, 142–45
Reserve Officer Training Corps, 105–6
(*see also* WAVES)

Velasquez, Loreta, 32–34

WAAC (Women's Army Auxiliary Corps), 12, 38–39
(*see also* WAC)
WAC (Women's Army Corps), 12, 38–40, 42–43, 74–91
basic training in, 74–77
enlisted specialties in, 77–80
officer candidate training in, 80–86
officer specialties in, 87–88
(*see also* WAAC)
WAF (Women in the Air Force), 54–73
basic training in, 54–59
enlisted specialties in, 59–65

officer candidate training in, 66–69
officer specialties in, 69–73
War of 1812, women in, 28, 32
WASP (Women Airforce Service Pilots), 42
WAVES (Women Accepted for Voluntary Emergency Service), 38, 40, 42–43, 92–109
basic training in, 92–94
enlisted specialties in, 94–102
officer candidate training in, 102–6
officer specialties in, 107–9
Weather observers, in the Air Force, 59–60
Weather officers, in the Air Force, 70, 72
Westmoreland, William C., 10
Women in the Armed Forces:
in 1949, 14
in 1970, 15
in 1978, 47
Women Marines, 110–25
basic training in, 110–12
enlisted specialties in, 113–17
officer candidate training in, 117–19
officer specialties in, 120–22
(*see also* U.S. Marine Corps, Women's Reserve)
Women's Armed Services Integration Act, 13–14, 43–44, 45
World War I, women in, 35–37
World War II, women in, 38–43

Yeomanettes, 36, 37

Zumwalt, Elmo, 94